Secrets of Lucky People

A Study of the Laws of Good Luck

Steve Gillman

Outskirts Press, Inc.
Denver, Colorado

The opinions expressed in this manuscript are solely the opinions of the author and do not represent the opinions or thoughts of the publisher. The author represents and warrants that s/he either owns or has the legal right to publish all material in this book.

Secrets of Lucky People
A Study of the Laws of Good Luck
All Rights Reserved.
Copyright © 2008 Steve Gillman
V4.0

Cover Photo © 2008 JupiterImages Corporation. All rights reserved - used with permission.

This book may not be reproduced, transmitted, or stored in whole or in part by any means, including graphic, electronic, or mechanical without the express written consent of the publisher except in the case of brief quotations embodied in critical articles and reviews.

Outskirts Press, Inc.
http://www.outskirtspress.com

ISBN: 978-1-4327-2236-4

Outskirts Press and the "OP" logo are trademarks belonging to Outskirts Press, Inc.

PRINTED IN THE UNITED STATES OF AMERICA

Introduction

There are people who seem to lead a charmed life.

Some of these lucky people aren't even very intelligent or skilled, and yet they seem to almost stumble into success. They have opportunities open up for them all the time. Things are handed to them. They win in the stock market, find their dream job, and get married to their ideal partner.

Then there are those who might joke that "If it weren't for bad luck I'd have no luck at all."

These are the perpetually unlucky people. You may know a few. They always seem to be unlucky in love, lose money when they invest, miss all the opportunities, have unexpected bad things happen, and generally struggle to gain any advantage in life.

Most of us are somewhere between these two extremes.

We have our share of "good luck". We have our share of "bad luck." We may never really know why, or whether there is something to be done. There is! That's why this book was written.

But Is Good Luck Really Something Else?

What about the whole concept? Is there such a thing as either good or bad luck, or is there another explanation? Is it just hard work? Are we somehow "cursed" or "blessed"? Or is "luck" just a lazy way to define the process of cause and effect?

Who cares!

You know it when you see it, right? To actually have good luck is more important than having an explanation or definition of it. The first lesson then, is that it is more profitable to make good things happen than to argue about definitions. The things you can do with this information will earn you the title of "lucky" even if you feel that "luck" had nothing to do with it, but don't sweat the label. Good results are good results, whatever they are called.

Now let's get started with a look at what lucky people are doing differently from others, and how you can have good luck too.

How To Use This Book

Before I started writing the introduction to this book, I went online to various search engines, to search the keywords "how to have good luck," "lucky guy," and "bad luck." What did I find? Web sites full of silly superstitions, lucky charms, and advice like "carry an acorn to ward off lightning" (no joke).

Hmm...

I haven't been hassled by lightning much, and I'm not into superstitions, so I hope you aren't looking for that kind of material here. This book is about practical, understandable techniques. Read it and you will know how to have good luck. Apply what you learn and you will be luckier.

Here are the basic premises:

1. "Lucky" people are those who have more happy

surprises in their lives, and more good situations in general.
2. Their results are because of the way they think and act.
3. With the powerful techniques and exercises here you too can use these principles or "laws" of good luck.

Getting Started

We don't all learn in the same way. You may want to read the book through in one sitting. Or you may want to take it in a little at a time. You might just scan it and return to chapters that interest you. If you first want to prove to yourself that the techniques here can work in real life, you can simply pick out a couple of the exercises and give them a try.

Use the book how it works best for you, but to develop new habits and a new mind set that perpetually brings more luck into your life, at some point you should probably get systematic about it. Then you should try to concentrate on one chapter at a time, perhaps for a week each. Think about the lesson, look at life to see if it makes sense, and do the exercise that follows it.

Apply what you learn here and you will be luckier.

Table of Contents

Chapter	1	Dave The Lucky Jerk	1
Chapter	2	John's Lucky Auction	9
Chapter	3	He Gave Them The Business For Free	14
Chapter	4	Howard, Hank And HUD	22
Chapter	5	Beyond The Surname Experiment	27
Chapter	6	Susan's And Sally's Party	32
Chapter	7	Eric The Smiling Bartender	36
Chapter	8	Chuck The Unlucky Real Estate Agent	40
Chapter	9	The Prospector's Reticular Cortex	46
Chapter	10	He Made $80,000 Playing Roulette	55
Chapter	11	Kentucky Fried Effort	64
Chapter	12	Getting Robbed On A Bus	69
Chapter	13	Miss A Flight, Make A Billion	77
Chapter	14	Don't Worry, Be Lucky	85
Chapter	15	The Dirty Mechanic	98
Chapter	16	Sometimes Thorns Have Roses	104
Chapter	17	My Lucky Flat Tire	110
Chapter	18	Gorillas And Lottery Tickets	117
Chapter	19	How To Buy An Island For A 94% Discount	126
Chapter	20	The Illiterate Millionaire	131
Chapter	21	The Lazy Investor	136
Chapter	22	Your Plane Crash Survival Story	143
Chapter	23	Ronald Reagan's Secret	150
Chapter	24	Thomas Edison's Secret	159
Chapter	25	Donald Trump's Secret	167
Chapter	26	Richard Branson's Secret	181
Chapter	27	Ben's Bad Luck Turns Good	192
Chapter	28	Imagining A Business Into Existence	199
Chapter	29	Climbing Mount Everest	206
Chapter	30	Mico Staring At The Sea	214
Chapter	31	George's Best Excuses	226
Chapter	32	Bad Luck Bart Blames The World	233
Chapter	33	The Great Ice Cream Opportunity	243
Chapter	34	The Unlucky Expert On Luck	253
Chapter	35	A Collection Of Luck-Boosting Ideas	258

Chapter 1
Dave the Lucky Jerk

The Results Of Courage

You gain strength, courage, and confidence by every experience in which you really stop to look fear in the face. You must do the thing which you think you cannot do.

- Eleanor Roosevelt

Many years ago, I used to work with a bunch of single men. One, whom I'll call Dave, was not well liked by the other guys at work. This was due in part to the fact that he was a jerk. Not to pick on him too much (sorry Dave), but he was rude, cocky, and he frequently lied to those around him. There may have been a bit of envy that played into the other's dislike of Dave as well.

You see, Dave seemed to easily get dates with many of the beautiful women in the area. This was a mystery to many. How could a jerk go out with all the women whom the other guys could only dream about?

We may wish it was true that you have to be nice to get lucky, but it isn't. Although he may have done even better if he was a nice guy, Dave did well enough for a simple reason: Because he asked women out! Most said no, but he just kept asking, until some of them said yes. He got lucky because he chose to face the fear of rejection, and keep on asking.

Aren't lessons like this common in life? In this case the answer was right there in front of the other men, but they didn't want to face the fear. We wonder at the success of others, when the key is that they're simply doing the things we're afraid to do.

Well guess what? They are afraid too! But they choose to act anyhow. The result? They get lucky.

Who is more likely to get a date? A man who asks out one woman or a man who asks out ten?

Who is more likely to get a raise at work? A woman who just quietly does a good job, or one who does a good job and asks for a raise?

You have to have the courage to do something if you want the results of that action. Obvious stuff, right? I had to start this book with an obvious and simple lesson for two reasons. One, because we sometimes need to be reminded of what we already know. Two, because sometimes the simplest principles, when actually put into practice, are the most powerful.

Feel The Fear And Do It Anyhow

Men of action are favored by the Goddess of luck.

- George S. Clason

Recently, I was at a free money-making seminar, and the speaker asked the audience if any of them wanted a hundred-dollar bill. A few hands went up. Then he asked,

~ Secrets of Lucky People ~

"Now who is actually going to come up here and get it?" Only a few people out of hundreds approached the stage. He handed the bill to the first one there, while the crowd sat watching, too afraid to embarrass themselves.

Exactly why did this one man get the hundred dollar bill? Simply because he walked up and took it, while the others took the advice of their fear.

We can see that fear gets in the way of having good luck. What can we do then to have more courage? There are self-improvement products, such as seminars and tapes and books that can teach us techniques for overcoming fear. These things can certainly help.

But a more immediate way to overcome fear is to simply start acting in the face of it. Start with small steps and work your way up. You can't wait until the fear is gone to act. Courage is being afraid but acting anyhow. The more you do this, the more you see that courage is not a precursor of action, but a result of it. Things get easier when you routinely do them.

Letting fear make decisions is a bad habit that is sure to get in the way of having more luck in your life. Acting from fear also sabotages your self-growth. Did you know that Johnny Carson had stage-fright every night before he went on the air? He stepped out there anyhow, and enjoyed doing the Tonight Show for decades. Fear is just a feeling, and you can move forward despite it.

Question your habitual following of fear's advice. Are your fears really looking out for your best interest? Are they pointing to real danger, or to small and even imagined risks? Ask for advice of your better self, and act on it.

Some more specific steps you can take:

- Talk to people who intimidate you.
- Ask for things from employers.

- Speak up in a conversation when you have something to say.
- Purposefully seek out things that make you nervous and do them, until it is a habit.

Try these simple things and you'll find that you can eventually motivate yourself to do even things that terrify you.

You Are Not Your Fear - A Deeper Understanding

If you really want to lead a more fearless life, you have to tap into your fearless self. Let's look at what that means.

To begin with, we can see that fear is normal and sometimes useful. If a bear is about to attack you, fear causes a physical reaction which makes it possible for you to run faster and fight harder. In this context, when the danger is real and immediate, fear can be good.

Fear, then, is a survival mechanism from our past evolution. However, it is much rarer today to face an actual and immediate danger, yet we probably feel as much or more fear as our cave man ancestors. What are we afraid of?

We are primarily afraid of the thoughts and images in our minds. For example, a man may think he is in fear of losing his job, but losing the job is not the cause of his feeling. After all, if he was fired one day with no warning, he would have no reason to be afraid prior to that, since he didn't "see" it coming.

The problem is that he does "see" it coming, whether it really comes or not. He thinks about the possibility, imagines the consequences, and has thoughts like, "What will I do? Will I lose everything? How will I pay the bills?" Then he looks at these thoughts like they're a bear stand-

~ Secrets of Lucky People ~

ing in front of him. Naturally he is afraid, even though he created the fearful image, and he could have chosen not to create it.

To use the example of the jerk who got the dates, the other men were afraid of scenarios their own minds created. They imagined the rejection, perhaps humiliation. The more imaginative may even "see" others laughing at them in their own minds. But what real danger did they face? It is only these ideas they were seeing that explains the fear.

Even in cases where there are real risks, the danger is often not immediate, so the actual fear response is not appropriate. For example, you could spend your days terrified because you are going to die within 50 years or so, but you won't get any benefit from such a fear. You may even die sooner as a result of the constant stress.

Nonetheless, we do regularly worry about the future. This is one of our most common fears. It's true that if you start a business you might fail, but this is not an immediate danger, and the anxiety, stress and panic caused by focusing on everything that can go wrong does more harm than good. It often prevents us from moving forward in life.

When we see this, the question naturally arises: How do we stop the fear which keeps us from doing what we want and what we need to do?

The bad news: we can't stop fear. The good news: we can understand it and stop taking its advice. We can see that there is a part of us that creates fear, that imagines the worst and holds it up for us to see. It reminds us of the ways we may fail, and though its predictions are usually wrong, it can still scare us into inaction or inappropriate action. We all sometimes listen to this part of us, and consider it to be our own internal voice.

It isn't.

Imagine if a fearless spirit took over your body, and

used your brain and skills and knowledge. Because it doesn't identify with those fearful thoughts as its own, it doesn't act accordingly. It hears them, but dismisses them as unimportant. Such a spirit could do much more than you, right? It would have the same body, brain and situations - and even the same fearful thoughts - yet be able to act without fear holding it back.

As we ponder this, some part of our minds might say, "We need to consider what might go wrong so we don't make mistakes!" That is again the fearful part of us, which now wants us to worry even about not worrying. But you don't need negativity and anxiety to see danger, and to take precautions. You can be rational about that. And to worry about not worrying is a bit ridiculous, isn't it?

Now here is an interesting and useful thought:

That fearless spirit which inhabits your body is you.

When you think those demotivating thoughts are "you," you're just making a mistake. They are not you anymore than every silly or worthless thought that passes through your mind is you. To identify with that part of yourself is simply an error, and one you can correct. You can start to doubt those negative and fear-creating thoughts inside you.

If everything a friend told you got you into more trouble, would you keep listening? No? Then look at the results you get from following the advice of those fearful thoughts in your mind. They are not really trying to help you grow as a person, nor even to protect you, are they? They seem to be doing nothing but trying to perpetuate their own existence. See it that way, and you might be less inclined to listen to them.

Watch the process from this new perspective, and you'll come to doubt those thoughts which only seek to create fear. When a fearful thought or image arises, you'll start to think, "This is just an idea, and not a very useful

~ Secrets of Lucky People ~

one. I'm going to see what happens if I ignore it." Then you can act on what you see as right, not on the advice of those fearful thoughts. Confront any discouraging ones with questions like "What if you are wrong?"

The power of these demotivating imaginings will diminish the more you question them and replace them with better thoughts. You'll probably always have fearful interior voices giving you "reasons" to not go for your goals. But with honest self-inquiry and a bit of understanding, they will become less powerful.

Luck Exercise

List five good things you have hesitated to do because of fear, nervousness, or discomfort. These can be as simple as saying hello to someone, showing a story you wrote to another writer, signing up for a dancing class or asking for a raise at work.

Once you have your list, pick an item and see what thoughts arise as you anticipate doing it. Question any thoughts which discourage you. See that they are not your true voice nor your protectors. Then just do the thing as soon as you can, even if you are shaking with fear.

Did you do some real damage to yourself by doing the thing that scared you? If not, make a note of that (at least mentally), and remind yourself of this the next time you face a scary situation.

Pick another item to do the next day or the following week, and work your way through the list in this way.

1._____

2._____

3._____

4._____

5._____

The important thing is this: To be able at any moment to sacrifice what we are for what we could become.

- Charles DuBois

Chapter 2
John's Lucky Auction

Being In The Right Place

Location, Location, Location.

- Proverbial Real Estate Investing Advice

Where you are matters. In fact, it is sometimes said that good luck is simply being in the right place at the right time. Fortunately, you can choose to be in these right places at these right times.

When I was younger, I had a friend, Mark (not his real name), who was always talking about how lucky some people were, and of course about how unlucky he was. (It's amazing how often people say this as though they are proud of it.) One day he came to me and told me "Did you see that truck John just bought for $2,000? It must be worth at least $6,000 or more. How does he always find those deals?"

John bought and sold used cars, and often found good deals. I mentioned to Mark that John bought it at an auction, where the cars often sell for less. In other words, he was in the right place. I pointed out to Mark that since it was a public auction, he could have been there as well.

"I went to that auction once," he answered, "but I didn't see any deals like that." John goes almost every other week, I patiently told him, so of course he's more likely to be there at the right time to get the best deals. He's so lucky that way.

That could be the whole lesson. Just go where the action is, and go there often. But in case it didn't sink in, I'll ask a few questions to encourage you to apply it to your own life:

- Where are you more likely to get a "lucky break" as a movie star: in Clinton, Ohio, or Hollywood?
- Will you have better luck in love at a party, or staying home watching TV?
- If you want to be a great skier, should you move to Florida or Colorado?
- If you want to learn how to invest in real estate, should you spend time at the bar or with a real estate investing club?
- Is a thrift store or a rent-to-own store a better place to save money on your furniture?
- Will you have more luck with your writing showing it to friends or to writers, agents and publishers?
- Will you meet more business people at a bar or at a financial seminar?

Choose To Be In The Right Place At The Right Time

A few years back, my wife and I spent a winter in Tucson, Arizona. Over the course of two months I read about 40 books on real estate investing, but we rarely went out to look at properties. Although I have invested in real estate over the years, to be honest, I prefer to talk about it and

~ Secrets of Lucky People ~

read about it. Not surprisingly, we didn't find anything to buy.

The next year, when we moved to Tucson, we joined a local real estate investors association. We mentioned that we were looking for a fixer-upper to invest in, and it took just three days for someone to call us with a deal. We didn't even have to go find a property ourselves. That is the power of being in the right place.

Another example: Magician David Copperfield was making more than 40 million dollars per year by the end of the 1990's. As a child in New Jersey, however, his family had so little money that he had to share a bedroom with his parents. How did he become so wealthy?

There are certainly many reasons for his success. He puts on a great show, as we discovered recently in Colorado Springs. But the relevant lesson here is that he made it a point to be where he needed to be. He snuck into Broadway shows, for example.

He also started to spend a lot of time hanging out in Tannen's in New York City. Tannen's is the world's largest magic shop - not a bad place to be if you want to be a magician. Soon after he became the youngest person ever accepted into the Society Of American Magicians.

Right Place Equals Right People

When you are determining where the "right place" is, think in terms of where the "right people" are, and when. If you want to become a stock broker for a large firm, it could help to move to New York, of course. But it can also help to find out which bars the brokers spend their time in, and when. It is people that make places matter.

Here are some more examples, just to get you thinking:

- If you want to succeed in a local service business, join the chamber of commerce and go to the networking events.
- If you want to get to know wealthy people, volunteer for their favorite charities - at least the ones that they personally get involved in.
- If you want to fish in the best places, see who has the most fish on their stringers and watch where they go, and when they go there.
- If you want to improve your speaking skills, find out where and when the closest Toastmasters International club meeting is held.
- If you want success with a new coffee shop, count how many people drive or walk past prospective locations, and choose one with a lot of traffic.
- If you want more friends, get out of the house and go somewhere.
- If you want success in anything, find out where other people who are successful in that area of life "hang out," and then go there!

Luck Exercise

List several goals you have. If you are not sure that something is a goal yet, list it anyhow, just for practice. Then after each goal, write down one or more useful places you can go to that will make realizing that goal more likely.

The Goal: _____

The Right Places: _____

~ Secrets of Lucky People ~

The Goal: _____

The Right Places: _____

The Goal: _____

The Right Places: _____

The Goal: _____

The Right Places: _____

The Goal: _____

The Right Places: _____

Be where the luck is.

- Steven Scott

Chapter 3
He Gave Them The Business For Free

Preparation For A Lucky Life

Luck is what happens when preparation meets opportunity.

- Seneca

You have probably heard the saying that "opportunity only knocks once." I say it knocks a thousand times. Unfortunately, we often don't listen, we don't answer the door, or we don't want to work. The biggest problem, however, includes all of these and more: It isn't really an opportunity if you aren't ready for it.

My friends Sam and Jessica (not their real names) had a business handed to them for free. Yes, it was a business that actually made some money, and they paid nothing for it. It was a small packaging and shipping business in a Midwestern town where they lived.

The business made a profit every month. Not a lot, but there were many ways to improve it and make more money. The owner simply didn't want to deal with it anymore, because he had other things going on in his life (presumably more profitable things). However, he couldn't just close the doors and call it quits, because he was still obligated to pay the lease on the building for almost another year.

This is where my friends enter the story.

They listened, and let the man explain his situation. Listening to people is a great idea if you want to have more luck.

They looked at the business, and saw the potential. You have to recognize an opportunity to take advantage of it, right?

They worked, doing what it took to benefit from their "good luck." For example, they added a copy machine and a resume service to the business. You may have heard the saying, "The harder I work, the luckier I get."

The owner agreed to give them the business if they would simply take over the lease on the building. You can see some of the reasons for their good fortune. The biggest reason they "got lucky," however, includes the others, and goes beyond them: They were prepared.

How were they prepared? They had a little bit of money saved to handle the transition. They also had experience with a small tax preparation business of their own. They were willing to learn what they needed to learn. Honestly, if they had no money and no business experience, they probably would have had to let someone else take the business.

A Bad-Luck Example

Remember my friend Mark's comment about how lucky John was to get a $6,000 car for $2,000 (previous chapter)? Well, there is more to that story.

John is one of those people who is naturally and almost

impulsively generous. When he heard about Mark's interest in buying and selling cars, he offered to sell this $6,000 car to him for $3,000. He would be happy to make a quick $1000 profit and happy to see Mark sell the car for a profit of $2,000 or more (after taxes and other costs).

Did Mark jump at this opportunity? He might have - although unlucky people often hesitate and over-analyze things when opportunities arise. However, his problem - I mean excuse - was that he just didn't have the $3,000, and couldn't think of any way to get it.

Look at this clearly. Despite all of his envious comments, he could have been "luckier" than John in this case, with a bigger profit on the same car. But he had to be prepared.

What could Mark have done to be prepared? I'm going to lay this out plain and simple, in case any readers out there are making excuses for Mark.

1. He could have saved the money to invest.

If he had started two years earlier, he would have needed to put aside $4.11 per day to have the $3,000 at this point. He also could learn from this mistake and start setting aside that money now for the future. He did neither.

2. He could have used a credit card.

He could have previously obtained a credit card with a high enough limit to handle deals like this. If it took him a month to sell the car, the 3% cash advance fee and 18% annual interest would have knocked just $135 off his thousands in profit. Of course he had to have the card ready beforehand.

3. He could have borrowed from friends.

He could have previously arranged with someone to borrow the money and split the profits when deals like this came up. I would have put up the money for half the profits if Mark had come to me. I had funded similar deals several times for other friends. He didn't ask.

These are just some of the things Mark could have done to be prepared for opportunities like this. Not having done any of these things, there was no opportunity here for him. He is so unlucky in that way - and unfortunately proud of this, rather than seeking to change it.

General Preparations For A Luckier Life

Luck favors the mind that is prepared.

- Louis Pasteur

Wherever you want luck to happen in your life, prepare. Aren't there always ways to be more prepared? If you want to be lucky in love, you comb your hair, right? If you want to have good luck in the stock market, start studying, start setting aside money to invest, and start exploring the possibilities.

There are endless examples of these specific preparations you should make, such as putting on a clean shirt for a job interview. Then there are the general preparations that can lead to luck in almost any area of your life. Here are some suggestions on these:

1. Set Aside Money

This may sound like a tough one, but you can do it. Consider for a moment that there are people living on less money than you - probably people you know. Why not live like they do for a while, and bank the money you save?

What if you really can't save any cash? Keep a credit card ready for any opportunities, or become friends to people who have money to loan. Money creates luck, in big and small ways. For example, is it lucky to see your favorite jeans on sale for half-price? Only when you have the money to buy them.

2. Set Aside Time

This isn't a matter of sitting around doing nothing while waiting for things to happen. I mean having the time available for opportunities that come up. If a friend calls to tell you that your favorite motivational speaker is in town, or he just wants to treat you to lunch, it is good to have the time available for these.

But how?

With good planning, you can still fill every moment of the day with activities and yet be able to take time out for any opportunities that appear. Just don't have too many time commitments. Plan as much as you want, but try to have time-specific tasks (meetings, for example) done early in the day, or all around the same time of day. If the other tasks can be moved around, you can often make room in your schedule to take advantage of unexpected opportunities.

~ Secrets of Lucky People ~

3. Get To Know People

There is more on the importance of people in several other chapters here, but the essential lesson is this: Knowing people means being connected to the world, and the more connections you have, the better your chances for good luck.

One day, a young man told me that his family needed to sell their home fast and cheap to avoid foreclosure. He didn't know what to do. That night I called a friend who invests in deals like this. He made a profit helping them, and the man's family got to stay in their house. This investor friend knows many people, so he probably gets plenty of calls like this, and makes a lot of money.

4. Always Keep Learning

Is Donald Trump lucky? He says he is, as do many others, so we might want follow some (but not all) of his examples. In his book, *How To Get Rich*, he says that he likes to read self help and psychology books. He also reads biographies, and about great philosophers.

One of Trump's continuing goals is to learn something new every day. I think this is a worthy goal for anyone who wants to have more opportunities in life.

5. Develop Good Luck Habits

In other words, read these lessons, apply them, and keep applying them until they are habitual. There will be more about habits - both good and bad - later in the book.

Luck Exercise

List several areas of life in which you would like to have more luck. Then, after each item on the list, write down one or more things you can do to be better prepared for any opportunities that arise. Start doing something from this list each week.

I Want Luck With: _____

Preparation: _____

I Want Luck With: _____

Preparation: _____

I Want Luck With: _____

Preparation: _____

I Want Luck With: _____

Preparation: _____

I Want Luck With: _____

Preparation: _____

~ Secrets of Lucky People ~

I Want Luck With: _____

Preparation: _____

By failing to prepare you are preparing to fail.

- Ben Franklin

Chapter 4
Howard, Hank And HUD

Know People For Better Luck

It's not who you know... well, okay it is who you know.

- Anonymous

This is another obvious, and yet often overlooked secret of good luck. Who do you know? Does it matter? Of course it does! Never mind if it should or shouldn't matter - it does.

Howard

Howard knew everything about investing in HUD foreclosures (HUD is the U.S. Department Of Housing And Urban Development). He had studied and studied. In fact he had bought six books on the subject and taken notes from every one of them. The idea was simple enough: buy the homes HUD forecloses on, then fix them up and resell them for a profit.

For some reason, though, he always seemed to learn about the next foreclosed HUD home too late. If he did get

~ Secrets of Lucky People ~

his bid in, there was always someone who bid a little more. "It's my usual bad luck," he told his friends, but he didn't ask why it was this way. He also didn't associate much with other investors or real estate agents. "Real estate isn't about people," Howard told his friends, "It's just a numbers game."

Hank

Hank wasn't all that educated, but he liked the idea of investing in real estate. When he heard about the possibilities in HUD foreclosures, he did what he always did: He looked for someone who was in the middle of the action. In this case, that was a real estate agent who handled most of the HUD foreclosures in the area.

He asked the agent for help understanding the system, and took him out to lunch. They became friends, and soon Hank had invested in his first HUD home. The agent let him know when listings were coming up, and what price they would likely sell for. After buying and selling his second HUD foreclosure for a profit, Hank decided he might finally buy a book about real estate investing, to see what else he could do.

Now a question: Are you acting more like Howard or Hank? Certainly Howard's study habits can be a great help. But interestingly, having better knowledge beforehand wasn't necessarily the best way to succeed. Hank is the one more likely to be known as a "lucky guy."

This isn't about name dropping, or unfair advantages. When a new listing comes in, the agent will naturally tell the people he knows about it. You would do the same if you were in his place, wouldn't you? If you want to sell your car cheap, for example, who's the lucky buyer going to be? Perhaps somebody you know?

Knowing many people is one way to put this principal to work. Any one of them might clue you in to a great job, or an opportunity to make money, or a place to buy something cheap, or whatever you are looking for. In other words, just having more friends and acquaintances increases your odds of getting lucky.

On the other hand, you don't have to know a thousand people. Just be sure you get to know the right people. If you want to be an actor, don't stand there after a play talking only to the usher. Introduce yourself to the director, or at least the actors.

Tune in to the people who are the closest to where you want to be in life. Think like Hank and look for someone who is in the middle of the action.

Give To Receive

It is always a good idea to have something to offer when you approach others who might help you towards your goals. If you wanted to be radio disc jockey, for example, you could volunteer to help with some charity event the station is hosting. Helping the station out is a great opportunity to meet some of the people who work there.

If nothing else, at least give the gift of your ears. Listen to people. They'll appreciate it, and someday they might help you. How? It could be in as simple and powerful a way as mentioning your name to a station owner who then hires you for your first job on the radio.

You could take the cynical view of this being a way to create a sense of obligation in a person. Certainly there is some evidence that this kind of manipulation works. But you can also approach it as innocent advertising of your-

~ Secrets of Lucky People ~

self. When you offer something to a person, he or she is more likely to remember you, and to have the impression that you are a "giver" and not just a "taker."

A Quick Review

1. Know A Lot Of People
2. Know The Right People
3. Give To People First, And You Might Receive From Them Later

Luck Exercise

Write down the names of some people you know who might help you towards your goals. Make a point to call, visit, or email each of them this month.

1._____

2._____

3._____

4._____

5._____

6._____

7._____

8._____

~ Steve Gillman ~

9._____

10._____

Every friend was once a stranger.

- Steven Scott

Chapter 5
Beyond The Surname Experiment

The Value Of Acquaintances

Friends and acquaintances are the surest passport to fortune.

- Arthur Schopenhauer

Know more people to have more luck? A lot of this is common sense, but common sense is sometimes proven wrong. Wouldn't it be nice if there was some research in this area? Well there is.

Professor Richard Wiseman, from Britain's University of Hertfordshire, scientifically explored luck for over ten years. He found that lucky people really were doing things differently than others. In regards to knowing people, one simple experiment stands out.

The "Surname Experiment" is simple enough that you could do it yourself with you and your friends. Simply make a list of common last names, perhaps by opening up your phone book and taking notes. Then, as you scan the list, count how many people you know on a first-name basis that have one of the surnames on the list.

Wiseman used just 15 names. He tested thousands of people, who had classified themselves as either "lucky," "unlucky," or "neutral." He found that 50% of self-identified "lucky" people knew 8 or more people who had one of the surnames. Only 35% of "neutral" people, and only 25% of "unlucky" people knew 8 or more.

(In case this is confusing, I'll point out that it isn't about knowing those with common last names. That's just a proxy for how many people an individual knows in general. It's easier to do it this way, than to actually have respondents list every possible friend and acquaintance. Statistically, if you know more people with the most common names, you know more people overall.)

There were twice as many high scores among the lucky people as the unlucky. That's a pretty dramatic difference, isn't it?

Of course, one could argue that this doesn't prove that getting to know more people will make you luckier. It could be that the preexisting "luck" of these people brings them more friends and acquaintances, instead of the other way around. This is the problem with any such study based on correlation alone.

But if we consider this for a moment, it seems likely that it works both ways. In other words, certain "lucky" types attract more friends, but choosing to have more friends also exposes one to more opportunities. Experience, if you let yourself have it, will almost certainly show you that creating more "social connectivity" in this way leads to more possibilities, and that you therefore *can* change your luck for the better by making more acquaintances and friends.

Friends or Acquaintances?

You might think it would be more helpful to have

friends rather than acquaintances. However, the research says otherwise. Take, for example, the study done by Mark Granovetter, on getting a job. Though it was done decades ago, the principles haven't changed.

Granovetter discovered that of the hundreds of professional and technical workers he interviewed, over half found their jobs through a personal connection. This isn't very surprising, and by itself it is a good example of the value of "networking," and of simply knowing more people. The interesting part, though, was how well these workers knew the "personal connections" that got them the job.

Less than 17% of those interviewed reported that they saw the contact person "often." Over 83% said they saw the contact person "occasionally" or "rarely." Essentially, it was discovered that people weren't finding jobs through friends, but through acquaintances.

This makes sense when you think about it. Suppose you are considering finding a new job. Your friends are likely to work with you or go to the same places, and to know a lot of the same things. In other words, you already know much of what they know, so information on new jobs which are available is more likely to come from outside your circle of friends.

This goes beyond jobs, of course. Consider movies and books you have never heard of before, or new ways to make money, or just new information and ideas in general. Where are you more likely to hear about them? From your friends, whom you already spend a lot of time with? Or from acquaintances that are in other circles and subcultures?

The lesson is clear. More than with friends, having acquaintances from many walks of life can introduce you to opportunities you wouldn't otherwise know about. In other words, they can help you get lucky.

~ Steve Gillman ~

The Person Who Knows Everything

Apart from knowing a lot of people, and having a lot of acquaintances that are in different social circles, there is one particular type of person that you should get to know: a maven. Commonly defined as "an expert," a maven is more than that. As described in Malcolm Gladwell's book, *The Tipping Point*, a maven not only knows all about something, but is willing and eager to share.

You may or may not have met a true maven. They are people who can, for example, tell you where to get the best deal on almost anything. But more than that, they want to tell you. Some might also know exactly what the weather forecast is, and what new businesses are coming to town and when. They are fonts of knowledge, and live to share it.

Mavens have the ability to connect you with information and people that you need. When you mention that you are looking for a used car, a maven might know where you can get exactly what you are looking for, and at a great price. A casual mention of a book you are writing might get you the phone number of an agent who can help you.

Mavens are great people to know if you want more luck. If you meet such a person, make it a point to stay in touch with him or her.

Luck Exercise

List people you know who each operate in different circles or subcultures. Don't put two people on the list who work at the same place or even in the same industry.

Ideally, each person on the list should know a different group of people than the others. If you don't know a person's name, write a description and where you know him or her from. If you can't list at least ten, it's time to make some

~ Secrets of Lucky People ~

new acquaintances to fill out that list.

Make a point to contact one of the people on the list who you haven't talked to in a while. Buy the person lunch, perhaps, or just give him or her a ring to say hello. Invent a reason to call and stay in contact. Do this at least once a month with another person on the list. Start with any mavens you know.

1._____

2._____

3._____

4._____

5._____

6._____

7._____

8._____

9._____

10._____

Acquaintance softens prejudice.

- Aesop

Chapter 6
Susan's And Sally's Party

The Value Of Rapport

To listen is to tell them more about yourself than words can.

- Steven Scott

The party was dull, but almost all the employees made it, because they were expected to be there. Susan was off to one side, looking at the pictures on the walls. Though she was alone, the men were watching her because she was beautiful and single. She also knew more about the advertising department than anyone else there. That didn't seem to matter much, she thought to herself. No promotion in two years.

The boss had stopped to say hello, and she immediately began to tell him what she had been doing in the office that week. He left to talk to someone else. Others greeted her as well, but they wandered off as she went on and on about work.

Some of the men commented on how good she looked, and one also mentioned what a good job she did. "But she is

~ Secrets of Lucky People ~

always reminding us of all the work we have to do," he added.
Sally was overweight and never did dress very well, but people liked her. She stopped as soon as she entered the party to talk to one of the new employees - to see how things were going for him. Later she questioned one of the men about his wife and kids. When the boss said hello, she asked him how his vacation went. When he mentioned going sailing, she asked him how he had learned to sail.
She always had a genuine interest in others, and though they never noticed, she let them do most of the talking. Before long the boss started mentioning things about work. Sally occasionally suggested an idea or two, but mostly listened, and asked questions. The boss later told his wife, "I think it's time to find a better position in the company for Sally."
The next week, Sally got the promotion, and Susan wondered why.

Building Rapport

To get the most benefit from knowing people, you have to have some rapport with them. There are techniques for this, of course, and the simplest one is to ask people about themselves. Then listen! If your memory is poor, take notes (perhaps not right in front of them, but soon after talking to them).
Think about it, and you'll understand how powerful this can be. Imagine for a moment that you have just met two people at a party. You were introduced to both previously, but you don't really know either one very well. The first man says "Hi. How are you doing?" It seems that he doesn't even remember your name.
The other man walks up and calls out your name. He

then shakes your hand and says, "How did that stay at the cabin on the lake go?" You recall that you had mentioned the trip the first time you talked to this man. He waits for an answer, like he really wants to know.

Which man are you likely to talk to? And which one is more likely to get some useful information from you? For that matter, who would you be more likely to do a favor for? The one who apparently doesn't even remember your name, or the one who seems to have a genuine interest in you?

The second man understands the power of showing an interest in people. And though he may get some advantage from knowing how to talk to you, he probably truly wants to know how your fishing trip went. It isn't too difficult to be interested in people if you try. Of course, to show that interest, you have to know something about the person.

The first time you meet someone, learn a few personal things about him or her. Ask a few questions. Then write some notes next to the person's name in your planner or card file when you get home. Here is a short list of some of the things you might want to ask about.

- Does he have kids?
- What kind of pets does she have?
- Where did he vacation last, and why?
- What hobbies does she have?
- Is he involved in any social, political or business groups?
- Where does she live?
- Where has he lived in the past?
- What other jobs or businesses has she had?
- What is his favorite restaurant?
- What is her favorite sports team?
- What are his plans?

~ Secrets of Lucky People ~

It isn't as difficult as it might seem at first to get this kind of information in the course of a short and casual conversation. If you have just moved to town, for example, you can mention that fact, and ask the person you are talking to how long he has lived here. Along with his answer, he'll likely mention where he lived previously.

There is always something to be learned about a person if you listen, and it is worth the effort.

Luck Exercise

List five people you know, but not well. Make a point to get answers to the questions above from each of them, or from other sources.

1._____

2._____

3._____

4._____

5._____

The skills to drive a car may get you from here to there, but the skills of talking to others is what really takes you places.

- Steven Scott

Chapter 7
Eric The Smiling Bartender

Extroversion As A Strategy

Saying hello has a favorable risk/reward ratio.

- Steven Scott

Jack was looking over the records at his bar, and he noticed that whenever Eric was working, the bar seemed to make more money. Eric was a good bartender, he knew, but the difference in sales between his shifts and the others was not a small one. He checked on days when Eric covered for other bartenders, to be sure that he wasn't just getting assigned to the busier shifts. Sure enough, anytime Eric worked there was an increase in sales over what was normal.

He had to figure out why, so he sat at the end of the bar one evening and watched one of the other bartenders for an hour. He did a decent job as far as Jack could tell. Then Eric's shift started. There were about the same number of customers in the bar.

One man was sitting near Jack, almost finished with his sandwich and beer. From his body language it seemed the

~ Secrets of Lucky People ~

man was ready to leave. Then Eric looked over at him with a big smile. The man smiled back and said, "I guess I'll have another beer."

Jack chuckled. Was smiling the key? Could it be that simple? It was - almost. Eric smiled at everyone repeatedly, often with the same result as with this man. But in addition, if anyone was alone, he struck up a brief conversation. It didn't seem to matter what it was about. If customers had someone to talk to from time to time, they stayed longer, ate more and drank more.

Smiling and talking more. It sure was a simple explanation. Jack knew he was lucky to have Eric working for him. What he didn't know is that Eric made $120 more per week in tips than the other bartenders. He also didn't know that Eric was normally shy, but months before he had read about a study which proved more sales were made with smiles. Then and there he decided to give himself a raise.

The Research

In his research on luck, Richard Wiseman found that people who are classified as "lucky" by themselves and others, are outgoing, sociable people. No real surprise there, right? If you are outgoing, you are more likely to hear about opportunities in all areas of life. In other words, extroverted behavior can make you luckier simply due to the increased social interaction.

It's a numbers game: Meet more people to have more luck.

What does it mean to be extroverted? It can mean talking to people more easily, or being the first to introduce yourself when strangers gather, or purposely approaching strangers who may be interesting, just to say hello.

More specifically, Wiseman's research found that lucky

people smile twice as often as others. The research also showed that they engage in more eye contact than unlucky people do.

This lesson is really just an extension of the lessons on knowing people. The more you know, the better your chances of learning something new and useful, or of being introduced to some opportunity. Purposely choosing to engage in extroverted behaviors means you will meet more people and have more interaction with them.

Too Shy?

What if you are not an outgoing person? You could simply concentrate on the other ways to have good luck. If you apply half of the lessons in this book and ignore the rest, you'll still be far luckier in life.

Of course, even if you are normally a shy person, you can choose to be more outgoing in a given circumstance. In fact, the exercise below can help with that.

Luck Exercise

Make it a point to smile at people in circumstances where you don't normally. Strike up a conversation with a stranger, or someone you don't know very well. Say hello to people when you normally wouldn't. Over the next week, list six examples of actions like these.

(If you are an extroverted person already, you can probably skip this exercise.)

1._____

2._____

~ Secrets of Lucky People ~

3._____

4._____

5._____

6._____

How many opportunities are missed for the lack of a hello or a hand shake?

- Anonymous

Chapter 8
Chuck The Unlucky Real Estate Agent

Paying Attention

I think the one lesson I have learned is that there is no substitute for paying attention.

- Diane Sawyer

I will call him Chuck. He sat at the desk in front of mine at the real estate office where I briefly worked as an agent many years ago. He had been there six months and he hadn't sold a thing. He considered himself to be unlucky.

One day, an agent was on the phone explaining to a friend that he had to find someone to cover his "floor time." Chuck almost certainly heard the conversation, since I did while sitting further away. However, he just kept arranging his desk.

Floor time is the time agents spend taking the incoming phone calls. These calls are typically from people who saw a house they liked in a newspaper advertisement or real estate guide, or are coming to town to look for a house, or are otherwise interested in learning more about some property.

~ Secrets of Lucky People ~

Often these people don't have a real estate agent to work with yet.

Taking these calls is obviously a good way to make a sale and get a commission if you are new and have nothing more to do than straighten out your desk again.

Chuck could have offered to take the other agent's floor time, and possibly made a sale, but he was busy fiddling with his things. I took the floor time, and I did get a listing out of it, which later sold, making me a nice commission. Chuck quit the business a couple months later, having sold just one property during his entire real estate career.

The Price Of Good Luck - Pay Attention

Lucky people pay attention. They listen to what others around them are saying, and look for the opportunities in those conversations. The story above is certainly not the only example of this principle which I have seen or been a part of.

A friend of mine once bought a beautiful boat for half of what it was worth. How? He was paying attention when the owner mentioned that he needed to get rid of some of his "toys," and he asked him what he meant. The boat was one of the "toys" this man wanted to get rid of - cheap. My friend was often lucky like this, and he was always a good listener.

There are endless stories like these. I can think of many in my own life, and if you consider your own experience and that of your friends, you'll probably notice that some of the good fortune you and they have had came from paying attention.

How do you productively pay attention? Listening well helps, as does observation, but you could feel schizophrenic trying to watch everything and listen to everyone. It is better to just have a general awareness of what is going on around you, and what is being said, while being ready to "tune in" to those things potentially relevant to your pursuits. The following are some examples to get you thinking.

- An accident-lawyer's ears should perk up if someone mentions an accident they were in.
- A real estate investor should spot that run-down house with the un-mowed lawn, and write down the address.
- An internet entrepreneur should stop to read an article on new e-mail legislation or changes at Google.
- An art gallery owner should notice a beautiful mural on a building, or a good painting at a starving-artist show.
- A single man looking for love should spot the absence of a wedding ring on a woman's finger, and the presence of a smile on her face.
- A philosopher should find principles in action wherever he looks.
- Your dog should come running when he hears the refrigerator open.
- You should know what you want, and pay attention to anything that suggests opportunities to get it.

Take Notes

It is great to pay attention at the moment, but it helps even more to take notes. When my wife and I were involved with a real estate investors club, we noticed that some people often found deals before they are even listed

~ Secrets of Lucky People ~

for sale. Why? One of the reasons is that they had written down the phone numbers of many of the other investors, along with the types of properties each one dealt with. They would call them from time to time to see if there was anything they needed to sell.

Some Research

Are you lucky or unlucky? Richard Wiseman, from Britain's University of Hertfordshire, asked this question of lottery winners as part of his ten-year study of luck. He found that a person's perception of their own luck had no relation to their likelihood of winning. No surprise here, since lotteries are a matter of random chance.

(Perhaps this will be a great disappointment to those who believe our thoughts directly control the universe, but we are looking at techniques here that have evidence for them, not wishful thinking.)

In another test, Wiseman asked participants to count how many photographs were in a newspaper. On page two, in plain sight, there was a message in large block letters, which said "STOP COUNTING – THERE ARE 43 PHOTOGRAPHS IN THIS NEWSPAPER". It was formatted to look like an advertisement.

He found that those who described themselves as "lucky" were far more likely to notice the message. Lucky people look around, notice things, and then pay attention to those which are relevant.

Luck Exercise

List some things you overheard today. Alternately, just list some news you saw on TV, or some things that you noticed at work. These should be things that you would normally just forget about or place no importance on.

Now, after each item on your list, write a note or two about what opportunities might be found in this new information. What can you do with it? How could it be valuable? If you really see no usefulness or possible opportunity for yourself, make a note about how someone else might benefit from this information.

The point here is to train your mind. You are training it to both pay more attention to the things going on around you, and to look for the opportunities. Repeat this exercise regularly until your ears automatically perk up when you overhear something relevant, and you instinctively ask "where is the opportunity here?"

I Noticed Or Overheard: _____

Possible Opportunities Here: _____

I Noticed Or Overheard: _____

Possible Opportunities Here: _____

I Noticed Or Overheard: _____

Possible Opportunities Here: _____

I Noticed Or Overheard: _____

Possible Opportunities Here: _____

~ Secrets of Lucky People ~

I Noticed Or Overheard: _____

Possible Opportunities Here: _____

The capacity for delight is the gift of paying attention.

- Julia Cameron

Chapter 9
The Prospector's Reticular Cortex

Attracting Luck

Luck is believing you're lucky.

- Tennessee Williams

Two friends, Bob and Ken, took a week off work to go prospecting for gold in the Sierra Nevada mountains of California. They were working the same stream, just a mile or so from each other. One day, Bob's sluice broke, and the contents ran out onto the ground.

"My usual bad luck prevails," he sighed. He stared at the mess for an hour before walking upstream to tell Ken that he would have to head to town to buy a new sluice.

"Well at least it's an opportunity to get some more supplies," Ken told him. Bob grunted and got in the car. He drove up the dirt road, wondering what bad thing was going to happen to him next.

While Bob was gone, Ken's sluice broke as well. They had both bought the same kind, so perhaps there was a design flaw, Ken thought. He looked at the situation for a moment and laughed.

~ Secrets of Lucky People ~

"Maybe that was lucky," he told himself. "I was getting tired of working that thing." Then he remembered the gold pan he left in the bushes. He took it upstream to explore other areas.

He found a few flakes of gold and one small nugget in a new location, and made a mental note to bring the sluice there later, when it was repaired or replaced. He looked around, wondering what else he might find, because - as he reminded himself - he was always stumbling into some opportunity.

Soon he noticed that the ponderosa pine trees here produced the largest pine cones he had ever seen. He had a garbage bag in his pocket, which was quickly filled with the cones. He had seen similar ones for sale for three dollars each at a gift store they visited the day before.

When Bob returned, he saw the bag of cones and laughed. "What are those for?" Ken just smiled. He showed Bob the broken sluice, but Bob was looking at the gold pan, seeing the glitter of gold. "You always get so lucky!" he said.

"Yeah, I guess I do." Ken answered, and then he pointed out why the sluices broke. Bob looked at the one he had just bought - the same kind - and sighed, barely listening as Ken suggested how they might design a better sluice and sell them to other prospectors. Ken made some notes, and drove to town to get materials to rebuild his sluice.

When he returned, it was starting to rain. Bob looked at the sky and said "Now what?" Ken pointed out that rain loosens the gold hidden in dirt and rock crevices, and washes it into the streams. This would be good for them. He also explained what he was going to do to fix the sluice, and how he might sell the new design.

Then he mentioned that the woman at the gift store had just paid him $30 for his garbage bag full of giant pine cones. "It sure was lucky that the sluice broke," he added. Bob just looked at his wet pants, and sighed.

Would it surprise you to learn that Ken always had more luck than Bob? It is easy to see that he has a better attitude, and our experience tells us that this is important. Now let's look at why, and what we can do to think more like Ken.

The Reticular Cortex

While reading the book, *The Celestine Prophecy,* many years ago, I had a series of strange and lucky coincidences occur in my life. The book had a lot to say about such happenings, and the mystical reasons for them. I am a skeptic by nature, and to be honest, I couldn't buy into half of the ideas I was reading. Nonetheless, just by bringing the idea of lucky coincidences into my consciousness, the book did make me see them all over.

That's the power of our minds. But notice that no belief in spiritual powers nor mystical causes was required. All that was needed to change my experience of life was the mechanical process of looking at things a certain way.

What you focus on, and the ways in which you think about circumstances, affects your life. Finding opportunities because you choose to look for them is not "new age" nor mystical. It is simply effectively using your mind.

Another example: A while back, my wife and I were looking for a car. After some searching, we decided that a Chevy Astro Van would work well for our purposes. We wanted a used one at a good price, and only a few years old. With that intention in our minds, we began to see Chevy Astros all over. Of course they were there before, but now we were "tuned in" to them.

You have probably had a similar experience. When you

become aware of anything in life, and it is somehow important to you, you start to see more of the same all over. Do something as simple as counting the red houses you see this week and there will soon seem to be more red houses around than you ever would have guessed.

This is nothing mystical. It is due to the reticular cortex, which is a small organ in your brain, a kind of "gatekeeper" that directs incoming stimulus to your conscious or unconscious mind. Your thoughts more or less instruct it as to what to bring to your attention. This is why if you start studying flowers, for example, you might start seeing flowers all over that you never noticed before. You have effectively said to your reticular cortex, "Make me aware of anything about flowers."

To get the reticular cortex working for you then, you just have to focus on what you want. The more specific you can be in what your intentions are, the better. But just intending to do something, be someone or get something isn't enough. It does bring things into your awareness, but without subsequent action this is not much more than wishful thinking.

For example, once we were seeing those Chevy Astros all over, we still had to call the owners or car lots to set up appointments to test-drive them. We had to have the money set aside as well. I found a friend who knew about engines, so I would know we were getting a good car. We did these things, and bought exactly what we needed, and for 40% less than it was worth. That is the power of intention when it goes beyond wishful thinking to actions that make things happen.

Why Is This A Lucky Book?

Here's an interesting thought: Buying this book could

have made you luckier even if you never read it. Why? Certainly not because of some magical power. If someone hid the book in your house without your knowledge, it wouldn't affect your luck in the least.

On the other hand, your choice to buy it may have caused your mind to "tune into" the idea of having good luck, and instructed your reticular cortex to bring potentially lucky things and happenings into your awareness. You might have been "luckier" as a result. Of course, if you typically don't act to take advantage of new opportunities, this increased awareness may not help much.

A Lucky Mind Set

Sooner or later, those who win are those who think they can.

- Richard Bach

To develop the proper mind set, start counting all the ways you are lucky in life. You'll feel better, and a sense of gratitude is good for your soul. I don't mean this in a religious sense. Being thankful and noticing all the good things and happenings in your life affects your psychology. Just as you can depress yourself by dwelling on the negative, you can make yourself happier by dwelling on the positive.

Keep counting those blessings, and the next thing you'll notice is that you'll have more good luck. This won't be your imagination. I could tell you that God or the Universe will bring good things into your life once there is gratitude in your heart, but that's not my style. The truth is that this is simply how our minds function. It's that reticular cortex at work.

Acknowledging your good fortune, and watching for

more, creates the right frame of mind to take advantage of opportunities which otherwise might not be noticed. For example, a man hears about a new diet, and might normally think nothing of it. But because he's grateful for the good things in his life, and is watching for more, it catches his attention and he investigates a little. Months later and 30 pounds lighter he tells a friend "I sure was lucky to finally find a diet that works."

Seeing how fortunate you are, even if only in small ways, makes the possibility of good luck more real to you. This gets you watching. Then the watching gets you thinking, "How is this good for me? What can I do with this situation? Soon, with a bit of effort, you'll start to get answers.

Clearing Up Some Nonsense

You may recognize the ideas above as the "law of attraction" or "power of intention," both of which are hyped in many recent popular books. Unfortunately some authors are putting these out there as "absolute truths of the universe." Concentrate hard enough and you can "manifest" anything at all into existence, they claim.

You don't have to buy this nonsense. The right mind set can improve your odds tremendously, but it doesn't guarantee success every time. Of course, the "probability of attraction" isn't a very inspiring concept, is it? "Do this and you'll improve your odds of getting what you want" just doesn't sell books as well as "Do this and your success is guaranteed by the ultimate laws of reality."

But enough of poking fun at the mystical sellers of certainty.

There are two reasons I bring this up. One is that you have to do more than think about things and wish for results. You have to take action. This is glossed over by many authors. The other point is that if we see these things as absolutes, we give up too easily when they don't work. Nothing works all the time. Even your car may not always start, but you still get in it and try, because the odds are with you.

Start focusing on what you want then, because it does increase the probabilities of success, by putting the reticular cortex and subconscious mind to work for you. But learn what you need to learn as well, and do what you need to do to achieve your goals. The real secret of attraction is to get *your mind and your actions* working towards those goals.

Two Luck Exercises

1. Attracting Luck With Gratefulness

Write down all the things you are grateful for. Alternately, tell someone the many things you are grateful for. See if this simple exercise doesn't improve your outlook on life. It also helps to look over the list regularly, and to add to it from time to time.

1._____

2._____

3._____

4._____

5._____

~ Secrets of Lucky People ~

6._____

7._____

8._____

9._____

10._____

11._____

12._____

13._____

14._____

15._____

2. Attracting Luck With Attention

Spend a week with a notebook and pen on you. Jot down anything that happens which could possibly be called good luck. This will get you in the right mind set, which in turn will make you more likely to see opportunities you might have otherwise missed. You'll start to believe you're lucky, and that belief will alter your expectations and mind set in ways that will lead to more success.

The Luck Of The Week: _____

_____

~ Steve Gillman ~

_____
_____
_____
_____

You'll find good luck more often when you are looking for it.

- Steven Scott

Chapter 10
He Made $80,000 Playing Roulette

Working For Luck

It seems the harder I work, the luckier I get.

...?

The quote above has been attributed to Thomas Edison, Samuel Goldwin and others. It is almost the essence of this secret of good luck. Almost, I say, because it isn't as important to work hard as it is to work smart. How do you work smart?

Here's the short explanation: Decide what kind of luck you want, and work in that area or on that goal specifically. Do you want to stumble into a better job, and have your friends say, "Wow, that was lucky?" Then you need to be out applying for jobs. Is this simplistic? You bet, but simple principles are often the most powerful.

Even if you want better luck at a casino, there's work to be done. I worked at a casino for ten years, and I often operated the roulette tables. I watched thousands of people throw their money out there, just waiting for a "winning streak." Of course some did hit their "lucky streak," and then they usually lost the money right back. I only saw one man do the work necessary to consistently win.

Charting A Roulette Wheel

(The following is an excerpt from my e-book *You Aren't Supposed To Know - A Book Of Secrets*. It is a fairly detailed description of how one man won at roulette, which you can skip over if you like, without missing the point of this lesson.)

Years ago, I used to work in a casino. I dealt blackjack and sometimes poker. My favorite position, however, was running one of the roulette tables.

One of my players used to win regularly. When I ran the table, we would talk philosophy while he patiently made his simple bets all night. I knew he was winning, but didn't know how much. After I quit the job, I met him for coffee and discovered that he had made over $80,000 in sixteen months of part-time play.

In case you aren't familiar with roulette, here's how it works. The dealer or "croupier" spins the wheel in one direction, and the ball in the other. There are 38 "pockets" on an American wheel (1 through 36, plus 0 and 00). Players place their bets and are paid according to the number of the pocket the ball falls in. We'll ignore all the other various bets and concentrate just on the "straight up" bets - those on a specific number.

There are 38 pockets, and if your number comes up you get $35 for each dollar bet, plus you keep the bet. You can see that the house has an edge (5.6 percent, to be precise), but what if certain numbers came up more often than they should - more often than the expected 1-in-38 spins? That's when you can make money.

Let's suppose, for example, that number 5 is coming

up an average of once every 29 spins. If you bet ten dollars on it every time, you would lose 28 times, or $280, every 29 spins (on average), but win once, which would pay you $350. In other words, in the long run, you would be making $70 for each 29 spins. ($350 minus $280) When there weren't many customers, I sometimes did 60 or more spins per hour, so you can see that this could be very lucrative.

So why would that number or any other come up more often? The short answer is "Who Cares!" The longer explanation has to do with the nature of the wheels. The pockets could be manufactured imperfectly, with one or more slightly larger than the others, therefore catching the ball more often. One or more of the dividers between the pockets could be loose, meaning it absorbs the force of the ball instead of bouncing the ball away. The ball would therefore tend to drop into that pocket more often.

There are other reasons, including more temporary ones, like a drop of sticky pop in one of the pockets, or a build-up of dust. It isn't necessary to know what causes a "biased" wheel, though. The important point is that biased wheels exist, and can be taken advantage of.

Why would a casino let this happen? Roulette wheels are expensive, and so they are not often replaced, unlike cards and dice, which casinos replace daily. This means that if there is a bias, it can remain for months. I know for a fact that managers where I worked were aware of the problem with our roulette wheel. Apparently, as long as the table was profitable overall (most people lost), they weren't going to worry about one guy making money on it.

John (not his real name) came in initially with two friends, as he explained to me in the coffee shop. They took turns "charting" the wheel. This is nothing more than writing down the number that comes up on every spin. They did this for weeks on both roulette wheels in the casino. It is an incredibly boring, yet crucial part of the process, often amounting to nothing, since there may not be a bias.

You see, if the number eighteen comes up ten times in a hundred spins, it is meaningless. The sample is too small. You need to know if the bias is real, and therefore will continue, or is just a statistical fluke.

Without getting into probability theory and a discussion of standard deviations, suffice it to say that if you want to be fairly certain the bias is "real," you need a sample of at least 5,000 spins. They eventually had 15,000 spins recorded in a little notebook.

As it turned out, the number "0" was coming in 1-in-28 spins. This surpassed the 1-in-33 threshold they felt was needed to make it safe and worthwhile to bet on a number. So they sat there night after night, placing one bet on that one number, over and over.

Within a couple weeks, his friends had quit. They didn't have the patience required, and probably also didn't like the fact that even with the odds in their favor, they had nights when they lost as much as $700. Only John was willing to do this boring work (made less boring by large wins, of course).

So night after night John sat there discussing politics and philosophy with me and the other dealers, placing a $10 bet on "0" for each spin of the wheel. He was making between $50 and $100 per hour depending on the number of spins, and assuming the bias was consistent in the long run. Eventually, after more than a year, and $80,000 in profits for John, the casino finally got a new wheel.

To try this yourself, here is a simple formula:

1. Find a roulette wheel.
2. Write down the winning number for 5000 spins.

~ Secrets of Lucky People ~

3. Bet numbers which came up at least 151 times (1-in-33 spins).
4. If none came up that often, find a new wheel and start over.

"He's so lucky," the other players would say. Of course, they weren't playing the wheel twenty or thirty hours a week. They didn't bother to read about "biases" in roulette wheels. They didn't spend weeks writing down the results of 15,000 spins of the wheel in order to find that bias.

In fact, despite his obvious success, I never even saw any player do the simplest thing: copy his bets. His "lucky streak" came from doing the work they didn't want to do.

Doing The Work

Opportunity is missed by most people because it is dressed in overalls and looks like work.

- *Thomas Edison*

Thomas Edison had the good fortune to patent dozens of money-making inventions, but why? Perhaps because he kept working on new inventions. And why did the "lucky" roulette player in the above story make $80,000? Because he did the work necessary to understand the game and profit from a biased wheel.

But were Edison or that roulette player so fortunate in other areas of their lives? Were they lucky in love, or in sports, for example? I don't know. Maybe - or perhaps they weren't working on those areas of life as diligently. The point is: *You have to do the work where you want the luck.*

It's not that there is no random good or bad fortune in life. It's possible to win the lottery on the first try, or have a piano fall on your head, but you can't plan on these possibilities. What you can do, is work to put the odds more in your favor, to increase the number of times you "get lucky." Isn't that worth a little effort?

Luck Work - A Few Examples

- Want to be lucky in love? Read a book on how to attract the opposite sex. One good idea might lead you to meet your future spouse.
- Want to win more sweepstakes or other "pure chance" contests? Enter more of them and your odds of winning one go up. Find those that have fewer people entering, and enter those ones to put the odds more in your favor.
- Want to find better jobs? Get a better resume put together. Do some research to find out where the best jobs are. Practice your interview skills. Become better educated.
- Want to be in the right place at the right time? Start doing that luck-work: Find out where these places are and at what times it is best to be there, and then make plans to attend.
- Want to invest early in the next new business or industry? Start making contacts. Start saving money. Start doing research.
- Want to remain lucky in your relationships? Keep doing what needs to be done. Most of the things we value require ongoing work.

~ Secrets of Lucky People ~

A Look At Hard Work Versus Good Luck

Graham Green, the famous English writer, attributes much of his success to a habit: He forced himself to write at least 500 words daily, whether or not he felt like it. Creative inspiration can strike at any time, but it strikes more often when there is work instead of waiting. The same can be said of good luck.

But what is the difference between good luck and the results of hard work? Is there any difference? Maybe. My own preference over hard work is smart work combined with an open mind. I think that combination leads to more of what people call luck. Consider the following example.

A writer works long hard hours producing one great book after another. They don't sell too well, so he works even harder. He writes more and sends out more manuscripts to more publishers. Towards the end of his life he has built his writing career up to where it is a livable income. Hard work pays, right?

Now consider a writer with a more open mind, and perhaps a desire to do more than just write sixteen hours a day. He notices that good writing alone doesn't lead to success, and so decides to learn how to market himself and his writing. He starts a website to showcase his works, and he finds ways to get on talk shows and in newspapers.

He isn't always sure what to do, but he keeps trying new things and becomes a minor celebrity. A few years later a major publisher decides to capitalize on his growing popularity, and they contract with him for a series of books. Soon he is making millions.

"What a lucky break for a new author!" people say. It *is* a lucky break, but one which he helped create by working smart and keeping an open mind. This combination is even more effective than hard work, regardless of whether you call the results luck or not.

Luck Exercise

List some of the things you want out of life. After each item, list at least two things you can start working on in order to increase the odds of "getting lucky" in this area. Put a big check mark next to them as you accomplish or start each of these tasks.

I want to be lucky with: _____

Work that can help: _____

Work that can help: _____

I want to be lucky with: _____

Work that can help: _____

Work that can help: _____

I want to be lucky with: _____

Work that can help: _____

Work that can help: _____

I want to be lucky with: _____

~ Secrets of Lucky People ~

Work that can help: _____

Work that can help: _____

When I work fourteen hours a day, seven days a week, I get lucky.

- Dr. Armand Hammer

Chapter 11
Kentucky Fried Effort

Perseverance Pays

Continuous effort - not strength or intelligence - is the key to unlocking our potential.

- Winston Churchill

Why does the world have Kentucky Fried Chicken? Perseverance. This is one of the most important secrets of good luck or of success in general. Why did Colonel Sanders succeed with his fried chicken? Because after failing to sell his recipe and ideas to 900 restaurants, he kept on trying.

Can you imagine continuing to try for a "yes" after hearing "no" 900 times? Sometimes I think it helps to be a bit crazy to really hit it big in business. Even knowing the success Sanders had, I'm not sure I can recommend trying anything 900 times. But it seems clear that giving up after one or two tries is no way to get lucky.

~ Secrets of Lucky People ~

Why Perseverance?

Patience and perseverance have a magical effect before which difficulties and obstacles vanish.

- John Quincy Adams

If you aren't sure about this, you need to look around. How many successful businesses can you find with owners less intelligent than you? More than one, I'd guess. People often succeed from sheer perseverance.

Did you know that the average successful entrepreneur has failed in several other businesses? They just keep trying until they succeed.

For example, millionaire Dal La Magma failed at ten or more businesses, more than enough to make most people start looking for a steady job. But he just kept on trying, and his "Tweezerman Corporation" now makes millions selling stainless steel tweezers.

When I was selling real estate, I was told how lucky I was to get listings from "FSBO" (for sale by owner) properties, since the owners were usually hostile to real estate agents. The rest of the story is that I spent hours at a time calling potentially hostile owners, and kept going until I had some leads. The other agents wouldn't do this. Lucky for me, persistence pays.

I'm not saying you should blindly keep doing the same thing. If it doesn't work, start doing something else. Persist, but only in pursuit of your important values and goals, not in your methods. Note what works and what doesn't. Maybe if Colonel Sanders tried a few new things along the way he would have succeeded after 90 attempts instead of 900.

Remember the story in the chapter on being in the right

place, about how John got lucky finding that $6000 car for $2000? It wasn't just a lesson about being in the right place. John also kept going back to the auction. Persevere, and you'll have more good luck.

An Excellent Formula

All of us have bad luck and good luck. The man who persists through the bad luck - who keeps right on going - is the man who is there when the good luck comes - and is ready to receive it.

- Robert Collier

Here is an excellent formula for "wise perseverance," as opposed to stubborn repetition. It is borrowed (and modified slightly) from self-development coach Anthony Robbins:

1. Try and try again.
2. Note what works and what doesn't.
3. Try a new strategy based on what you learned.
4. Repeat this process until you succeed.

Simple formulas are sometimes the most effective.

A Note On "Trying"

In one sense, "trying" may be the surest way to fail. It is too easy to say "I tried." It's better to think of it as "doing" rather than trying. Just semantics, you may say, but words affect us powerfully. When we say we are going to "give it a try" we do not generate the same level of commitment as when we say, "This is what I will do."

~ Secrets of Lucky People ~

"Doing" something often requires many attempts and course adjustments along the way. Some consider these adjustments as "failures," but they are nothing more than necessary steps. Is the first step a failure because it takes 100 more to reach your destination? Of course not!

Edison tested hundreds of materials as filaments for light bulbs before finding one that worked. I suspect that in his mind he was inventing a light bulb, not "trying" to invent one. Perseverance comes from a true commitment to succeed, not from just "giving it a try."

Luck Exercise

List some things you have given up on. Then list some new things to try to achieve those goals. Choose one of these goals that still has value to you and start trying again, and again, and again.

I gave up on: _____

I could try: _____

I gave up on: _____

I could try: _____

I gave up on: _____

I could try: _____

~ Steve Gillman ~

I gave up on: _____

I could try: _____

Nothing in this world can take the place of persistence. Talent will not; nothing is more common than unsuccessful people with talent. Genius will not; unrewarded genius is almost a proverb. Education will not; the world is full of educated derelicts. Persistence and determination alone are omnipotent. The slogan "press on" has solved and always will solve the problems of the human race.

- Calvin Coolidge

Chapter 12
Getting Robbed On A Bus

Using Your Intuition

The only real valuable thing is intuition.

- Albert Einstein

Both my wife and I had a strong feeling we shouldn't get on that bus in Cuenca, Ecuador, but neither of us said anything about it until later. Ana sat down, but there was no room left for me, so I was packed in with the other commuters standing up.

Almost immediately I noticed the drunk pushing his way through the crowd, randomly going this way and that. I knew something was up, and instinctively reached into my pockets to check on my money. We had just visited the ATM that morning, and the $170 cash in my pocket was the most we had carried in one place during the entire trip. It was still there.

The old guy pushed against me like he was trying to find a place to stand comfortably. I checked my pocket again. Still there...

A few minutes later some space opened up near Ana,

and I went over to her seat. I reached in my pocket again, and it was empty. The other pocket was empty too. I hadn't felt a thing. The old drunk was still on the bus. I looked over at him.

"We've been robbed," I told Ana. "All of it." I grabbed the drunk by his sweater. Of course, he was no longer acting drunk at all.

At the next stop we got off, dragging the thief with us. A police officer appeared, and a crowd formed. The man was very sober now, pulling out his pockets and insisting again and again that he was innocent. He said we could search him if we wanted.

I did search him, but I understood now that his associate was long gone with the money, probably off the bus at a previous stop. It was a common ploy. This man's job had been to distract my attention and push me closer to the partner who actually removed the money and papers from my pockets.

Despite his begging, and the impossibility of getting the money back, we had the officer take him to the police station on his motorcycle while we followed in a taxi (paying with money from under the sole of my shoe). We filed a complaint, and he spent the night in jail, then was released for a lack of evidence in the morning. At least his fingerprints were on file.

We had both felt we shouldn't get on that bus, but why? Were we psychic? Not at all. We already knew that crowded busses were prime locations for pickpockets, and we saw that this bus was going to be very full. We saw the "drunk" man bumping into people, and knew it was suspicious.

We didn't think about these things consciously, but they registered in our minds, and warned us. Unfortunately, we ignored this intuition, and I was robbed.

~ Secrets of Lucky People ~

Of course, a strong hunch can be for irrelevant reasons too. If you were hit by a blue taxi as a child, you might have "intuitive" hunches not to get into blue taxis for the rest of your life. So how do you know when to trust your intuition?

More on that in moment. First, let's look at the other ways we can use our intuition. It's not just a subconscious warning device.

Luck and Intuition

Those who study luck find that self-described lucky people are more likely than others to make good decisions based on intuitive hunches. They listen to their gut feelings more. They also commonly work to improve that intuitive process, by meditating to clear their minds of other thoughts, for example.

But what is this thing we call intuition? Think back to when you had a hunch about something. That was intuition. It is simply your mind using more than what you are consciously aware of. You may or may not become aware of the reasons for your hunch or feeling, but whether conscious or not, your mind is working to help you.

Then there is what we call an "intuitive grasp" of things. This is an understanding of a subject which goes beyond what can be consciously explained. It is a common experience among scientists. My own chess game is very intuitive in this way, and so I often cannot honestly say why I made a move.

Perhaps it amazed some people when Grand Master Gary Kasparov was beaten by a chess computer. But what is more amazing to me is that he sometimes won. A computer, after all, is not like a human. It can calculate positions many moves further ahead than Kasparov or any human being can. How, then, was Kasparov able to beat it?

He did it with his intuitive grasp of the game. Experience allows him to combine analysis with a "sense" of which move is best. The same thing is probably happening when "lucky" poker players consistently win against more analytical players.

Developing Your Intuition

Often you have to rely on intuition.

- Bill Gates

Meditating to clear the mind of other thoughts is one way to immediately improve the quality of your intuitive hunches. In a moment you'll be introduced to a quick meditation you can use for this.

Gathering enough information to work with will also help. Remember the computer programmer's maxim: garbage in - garbage out (GIGO). When enough good information is in there, your mind will go to work for you with or without your conscious participation, so feed it well. Intuition is not a magical or psychic power. It is simply an unconscious use of what is already known and observed.

Watching it and questioning it can greatly improve the usefulness of your intuition. If I had asked myself why I felt bad about that bus, it may have occurred to me, "Oh yeah, crowded busses are a bad idea. I know that." If a man looks at his strong negative feeling about a taxi, he might say, "Oh, it's just my irrational fear of blue taxis." Get in the habit of paying attention to your intuitive feelings.

Notice in which areas your intuition works best. Are you always right about your hunches on stocks? If so, give a little credence to them. If your feelings about people are always wrong, don't follow them. If you can figure what circumstances cause your hunch to be right or wrong, do that. Just pay attention more, and you'll develop a kind of intuition about your intuition.

Recognize that intuition doesn't arise in a vacuum. Your skill, knowledge and experience determine its potential effectiveness. A weak chess player will never intuitively beat that computer. So learn enough about a subject, before you expect any good hunches about it - or before you trust the hunches.

Watch, and you'll have hunches and ideas more often.

Four Steps To Better Intuition

1. Look for it to encourage it.
2. Watch and question your hunches to learn when to trust them.
3. Give your intuition good information to work with.
4. Clear your mind to allow it to function better.

This last step can be accomplished with a simple meditation. Maybe learning to meditate intimidates you, but the following exercise will only take you a minute to learn and do.

A Simple Meditation

Breath through your mouth and you'll notice that it expands your chest. Breath through your nose and you'll notice how your abdomen extends. This is because nose-breathing causes the diaphragm to pull air to the bottom of your lungs, delivering a good dose of oxygen into your bloodstream and brain. It also relaxes you.

Breathing through your nose is healthier, and is the basis of this easy meditation. Just close your eyes, release the tension from your muscles, let go of your thoughts as much as is possible, and take four slow, deep breaths through your nose, paying attention to your breathing. That's it.

This isn't meant to get you into a deep meditative state. You are just trying to relax and clear your mind, to allow your intuition to function better. Now bring the subject at hand back into your consciousness, and see what feelings and ideas arise.

What About The Paranormal?

Many people are looking for paranormal explanations for luck, and for related phenomena like intuition and creativity. But why? There are good psychological explanations for why some people are luckier than others, which have nothing to do with ESP or psychic abilities. There are exercises that have been shown to improve one's luck whether or not we have a decent explanation yet.

Why do people need an appeal to the paranormal? Perhaps part of the reason is that if psychic powers could bring you luck, it would be easier than making changes in how you think and act. There is nothing wrong with looking for an easier way - as long as the search does not become an excuse for not taking the steps that are proven to work.

In Richard Wiseman's ten-year study of luck, he found definite differences between lucky and unlucky people. What he didn't find, however, was any indication of anything paranormal. He says, "I've found plenty of evidence of unscientific approaches to data, but have never come across a paranormal experiment that can be replicated."

~ Secrets of Lucky People ~

This is from a scientist who is open-minded enough to study "luck," and yet can't find one single study showing paranormal powers which can be replicated! In his own studies he found that lucky people were not any more likely to win the lottery. Of course not! It is random chance. On the other hand, people who are considered lucky can win more often in business or love or even artistic endeavors, because they are not relying on paranormal powers. They are thinking and acting in ways that promote a better outcome.

Luck Exercise

To encourage your intuition, it helps to notice it when it works. Make a list of times when you have had a "gut feeling" about something that turned out to be correct, or when you had a new idea that popped into your head and was useful. Look over the list from time to time and add to it when you can. See if your intuitive hunches don't become more frequent.

My Useful Intuition Example: _____

My Useful Intuition Example: _____

My Useful Intuition Example: _____

My Useful Intuition Example: _____

My Useful Intuition Example: _____

My Useful Intuition Example: _____

~ Steve Gillman ~

My Useful Intuition Example: _____

My Useful Intuition Example: _____

Intuition isn't the enemy, but the ally, of reason.

- John Kord Lagemann

Chapter 13
Miss A Flight, Make A Billion

Having The Right Perspective

If you view all the things that happen to you, both good and bad, as opportunities, then you operate out of a higher level of consciousness.

- Les Brown

In his book, *Screw It, Let's Do It*, billionaire Richard Branson has a great story about turning a problem into an opportunity. He and his wife were in the Virgin Islands, and their flight to Puerto Rico had been canceled. It would be a long wait until the next scheduled flight.

There were a lot of disappointed people, and they were all sitting around doing nothing. What could they do, after all, but wait until the next flight? However, Branson takes a different perspective on these things. He immediately started considering other options.

Soon, he found an available plane, and asked how much it would be to charter it one-way to Puerto Rico. He was told $2,000. Looking around at the number of people waiting, he did some quick math. Then he took a small chalkboard and wrote on it, "Virgin Airways." Below that he wrote "One way flight to Puerto Rico, $39."

Once 52 people signed up, he was making a profit. Although he didn't actually start his Virgin Atlantic airline until later, this was the inspiration. A problem is sometimes an opportunity. This one lead to the creation of a major airline - but only because of Branson's approach to the situation.

Perspective: Problems Are Opportunities

The way we see the problem is the problem.

- Stephen Covey

Luck-researcher Richard Wiseman found that lucky people use many psychological strategies to turn bad luck into good luck. They might automatically imagine how things could have been worse, for example, in order to eliminate any paralyzing sense of hopelessness in the current bad situation. They also look at what can be done, and concentrate on that.

Have you heard the saying, "If life gives you lemons, make lemonade?" That is the frame of mind of a lucky person. They are always asking motivating questions, like, "What can I do with this situation? Could this be lucky in some way? How can I make lemonade from these lemons?"

I have read that in Chinese, the same character is used for "crisis" and "opportunity." Maybe we should start using our own language differently. Think "opportunity" whenever you are tempted to see a "problem."

~ Secrets of Lucky People ~

Looking For Opportunities

In the middle of every difficulty lies opportunity.

- Albert Einstein

Here are a few examples to consider, to help you take a better perspective about "problems," which may be great opportunities.

- Missed a flight? What useful book or magazine can you read while waiting for the next?
- Financial problems? What valuable lessons can you learn to help you eventually become wealthy? Learn them well, and this experience could lead to writing a book to help others.
- Stuck on the highway in a blizzard? This could be your opportunity to exercise your mind playing a problem solving game with others in the car.
- Lost your job? This is often the catalyst for the luckiest changes in life. What better job, business or other activity are you now free to pursue?
- The movie you and your wife wanted to see is sold out? This could be a great opportunity to go to the bookstore/cafe and learn about something together while enjoying great coffee.
- Sick in bed? This may be the chance you've waited for to start writing that novel, or to watch that real estate investment video you bought and set on the shelf a while back.
- Car trouble? Maybe thinking about a new car is just the motivation you need to start getting control of your finances, or to start that weekend business.
- Unlucky in love? Today's failures may be very

lucky, if a more perfect match is in your future. You might also use the time alone to better prepare yourself for life with a partner.
- In jail? Do you know how many people have gotten a college degree in jail - a degree they probably never would have had otherwise? Time to study and learn new things is always an opportunity.

A Deeper Look At "Problems"

I have to put the word in quotation marks, because problems really are not what we think they are. For example, a man can call it a problem when he misses his bus to work, but the "problem" is primarily a matter of perspective. He has an idea about what "should" happen - in this case getting to work on time, and he sees this as the only acceptable outcome.

In other words, his attention becomes fixed on just the one possibility. Then, when reality (in this case missing the bus) is different from what he thinks "should" happen (getting to work on time), he is disappointed. He resists what is happening and is stressed as he scrambles to find a "solution" to his "problem." He may even imagine losing his job and the negative consequences which could come from that, thus creating more fear and pain.

The result? His mind is closed to the many other possibilities that exist.

In reality, the man is just standing there watching a bus go away in the distance, while the world around him is constantly changing and moving on. Is this actually a problem in a negative sense? Is it demonstrably bad? Only by the measures we choose to use.

It's true that he might lose his job. But what else is possible? Lets look at a few of the endless possibilities.

- He might catch the next bus.
- He might sit down and cry and lose all motivation.
- He might go find a better job.
- He might lose his temper and hurt people.
- He might take a taxi to work and have a good conversation on the way.
- He might get angry and in this state not see a car that hits and kills him.
- He might call in sick to work and do something fun that day.
- He might go home and spend the day worrying about everything.
- He might decide to buy a car so this won't happen again.
- He might get yelled at by his boss the next day.
- He might take the day off and explore new businesses he can start.
- He might use this opportunity to turn his attention to his own thought process which causes so much stress, and then with observation and self-work learn a better way to live.

We could go on. We could imagine a thousand possible scenarios, some which we would call good and some which we would call bad. But this isn't just an invention of ours. We can look at real life and see that there are actually and always infinite possibilities, and never just one problem which needs to be resolved one way.

Of course we purposely devise some problems we want to resolve, like math equations, goals we set, and new inventions. But when it comes to "oh no!" kinds of "problems," they simply exist because our minds habitually create them by comparing "what is" to what we think "should be." What is:

The man is simply standing there at a bus stop with a thousand possibilities before him, oblivious to almost all of them because he sees only his self-created problem.

Have you ever caught yourself thinking or even saying, "This isn't how it's supposed to be!" If so, you have a "supposed to" or "should be" version of reality in your mind, which makes you painfully resist what actually is happening or what actually exists. This is not only painful, but it gets you stuck on one possibility: resolving the problem you just created.

To clarify this a bit more: A broken leg is real. The pain is real, and the necessity of care for it to be healed is real. But these are simply the facts. It is thoughts, such as, "This never should have happened," and "Oh look at the terrible things this means," which make it into a problem. Rocks are hard and life ends, but we don't necessarily see these as problems because they are simply facts which we accept. The difference may seem subtle, but it is real.

Here is one more example to make this clear: A man might consider it an irritating or even terrible hassle if he has to walk two miles in the rain to get to work. And yet the same man might consider it a major pleasure to walk twenty miles through blizzards to get to the top of a mountain he has always wanted to climb. The reality alone does not describe a problem nor limit the possibilities: our mental approach to it does.

To be able to see opportunity in every problem, then, start doubting your old perspectives. Read this chapter again if that helps. Remind yourself that at every point in life, and when facing every problem, there are many more possibilities than you can even imagine. Which ones will come to pass? You can't know for certain, but you can open your mind and participate in creating the possible outcomes.

~ Secrets of Lucky People ~

Luck Exercise

What problems or "bad luck" have you had recently? List some examples. Then after each one, list some possible opportunity or good luck that may have been there in that situation.

Do this often enough, and you will train your mind to approach problems and bad circumstances in a new and more useful way. You will be training yourself to think like a lucky person.

Be careful if you're better at finding examples of bad luck than at turning them into examples of good luck. You don't want to focus on the "problem," but on the possibilities.

Problem Or Bad Luck: _____

Possible Opportunity Or Good Luck: _____

Problem Or Bad Luck: _____

Possible Opportunity Or Good Luck: _____

Problem Or Bad Luck: _____

Possible Opportunity Or Good Luck: _____

Problem Or Bad Luck: _____

Possible Opportunity Or Good Luck: _____

~ Steve Gillman ~

Problem Or Bad Luck: _____

Possible Opportunity Or Good Luck: _____

Each misfortune you encounter will carry in it the seed of tomorrow's good luck.

- Og Mandino

Chapter 14
Don't Worry, Be Lucky

Taking It Easy

Your mind will answer most questions if you learn to relax and wait for the answer.

- William S. Burroughs

The research shows that people classified as lucky have less anxiety. This could be one of those "which came first, the chicken or the egg" questions. Are you lucky because you are more relaxed or are you more relaxed because you are a lucky person?

Probably both are true, but a more relaxed approach to life leads to better results for many reasons that we can understand from our own experience. For example, who can really claim that they do their best thinking when anxious and worried? Who hasn't felt a lack of motivation due to stress? And you can see from your own experience that it is easier to be creative when you are more relaxed.

How, then, do you lessen the stress and anxiety in your life? How do you worry less? How do you relax more? Here are some suggestions.

~ Steve Gillman ~

How To Stop Worrying

This too shall pass.

- Ancient Proverb

Remember the quote above, and repeat it as necessary. Consider for a moment, any crisis or stressful event from your past, and how it is no longer the huge thing it was. Wouldn't it have been nice back then to have the perspective you have now?

Well, you can't change the past, but you can take away some of the "sting" of a current stressful event by imagining it from a future perspective, perhaps seeing yourself laughing about it ten years from now. You can approach all present stresses and worrisome events with the attitude that "this too shall pass."

Here are some other techniques that will help you to stop worrying too much.

Make A Decision

A sure way to reduce anxiety about an unresolved issue is to make a decision. Even making a bad decision is often better than doing nothing. You may immediately resolve the stress when you finally decide to quit that job, buy that couch, or make that phone call. Nothing can crowd and cloud your mind with anxiety quite so much as decisions waiting to be made. Just make them, and if they prove to be bad decisions, make new ones.

Take Action

Action towards a goal tends to diminish worry. Doing

nothing but thinking too much about a goal, especially if you dwell on the hurdles, will cause you anxiety and stress. Certainly you should plan well, but when planning drifts towards over-analyzing (often this is worrying in disguise), it's time to start doing something positive.

Confront Problems

To stop worrying when there are serious problems, confront them head-on. Years ago I had to sue someone over a business matter. I was worrying about it for weeks. I finally just filed the papers, got on the phone, and came to an agreement. My stress was gone. In fact, my anxiety dissipated as soon as I started acting, *before* the resolution. This is an important point.

Suppose a man tends to dwell on past losses. Maybe one such loss was an investment that cost him thousands of dollars ten years ago. Today he would probably suffer less from that memory than he would from wondering if he'll make it on time to a concert he is late for - and paid just $30 for. There is usually more mental pain in thinking about a possible future loss than in the loss itself, or in thinking about the past.

You see, it isn't the problems themselves, but the anticipation of them that causes the most anxiety. Deal with them head on as soon as possible, and resolve them to the extent you can. Once resolved in reality or even in your mind (since this is where the real issues usually are), you will be able to relax.

Mental Categories

When there are too many things going on in my head, I put them on lists and feel better. Maybe you've had similar experiences. If you're thinking too much about something, and you stop to schedule a time to work on it, it's easier to let go of it for now.

Put that phone call you have to make on tomorrow's list, and you'll feel less anxiety now. You're creating "mental categories." Just telling yourself, "There is nothing I can do about this until Monday," can put a worry into a category of "nothing to worry about now."

Other mental categories: "out of my control," "this is for later," "somebody else's responsibility," and whatever else works for you.

Stop Worrying By Meditating

Meditating can be a great way to relax and to stop worrying. More than 15,000 people have now taken a course in "Mindfulness-Based Stress Reduction," or MBSR, at the University of Massachusetts Medical School. The results there and in other studies around the country are showing that mindfulness can reduce pain and anxiety. (Some studies even demonstrate that mindfulness meditation can help relieve depression, and help with weight loss.)

The most common form of the mindfulness meditations being used is the simple exercise of paying attention. This is based on the Buddhist traditions in which meditators observe the busy thoughts of the mind (our "monkey mind") as well as the physical sensations in the body. Expect to see more studies on this in the near future.

Don't Listen To Your Worrying Mind

Is it possible to simply think, see what needs to be done, and do it without worry? Of course it is, and we can see this is true from our own experience. Once in a while at least, on a good day, this is how we operate.

Nonetheless, when it is suggested that we worry less, it is common to worry that we won't get things done then. In other words, we actually start to get anxious about not worrying! This kind of thinking perpetuates itself in your mind, as though it has a life of its own.

It does have a life of its own, but only to the extent that you feed it by giving it your attention. When you hear your own mind creating stressful thoughts, say, "I'm not going to buy that nonsense!" Follow that with better thoughts.

How To Relax

The time to relax is when you don't have time for it.

- Sydney J. Harris

Sometimes we need fast and easy stress relief. After all, complicated techniques or elaborate meditative practices might be just one more thing to be anxious about. Here are ten much simpler solutions. Try them out, and keep in mind which ones work best for you, so you can use them regularly.

1. Breath Deep

Try six or seven deep breaths through your nose, with your eyes closed. Pay attention only to your breathing, while letting the tension drain from your muscles. This is a "mini-meditation," and possibly one the most effective of these stress-relief techniques.

2. Interrupt Normal Routines

Talk to the crazy lady in the park, or eat your lunch outside. Get up and look around to find anything beautiful to focus on for a moment. Doing anything that breaks you out of your habitual patterns can often relieve stress.

3. Hug Somebody

Of course, giving a hug means getting one. As long as it's from somebody you don't mind hugging, this can immediately reduce your level of stress.

4. Watch Your Mind

Notice mental irritants lurking just below the surface and resolve them. Make the call that's on your mind, put things on a list so you can drop them, and generally let go of non-essential thoughts. Practice this mindfulness exercise, and it may become one of your favorite stress-relief techniques.

5. Take A Hot Shower

This relaxes your muscles, plus any break from more stressful activities can reduce anxiety. Some find that an alternating hot and cold shower is even more relaxing, but be careful with this one if you have a weak heart.

6. Listen To Relaxing Music

Have your favorite relaxation CDs in the car, in your office, or wherever you'll need them most. Play them whenever you are feeling stressed.

7. Laugh

Your experience shows that this helps you relax, right? So does the scientific research. So find the person who knows all the best jokes, or look for something funny in front of you.

8. Walk

Walking is one of the best stress relief techniques, especially if you have at least ten minutes. It is even better if you can find a pretty place to walk. If not, at least walk someplace new to you. A new environment (as long as it is safe) stimulates your mind, and takes attention away from stressful thoughts.

9. Leave The Room

Sometimes the things in the room or related to the room are triggering your stressful thoughts. This is especially true at jobs where there is a lot of tension. Try getting out for a little while.

10. Drink Chamomile Tea

Chamomile seems to have a calming effect on the nerves, although any hot tea without caffeine may help relieve stress.

Relax With The Situation

Researchers speculate that one of the reasons relaxed people have more luck is that their intuition functions better when they are at ease. You are also more likely to pick up on the body language of the person in front of you when you're relaxed.

Suppose you are applying for a job, and you're nervous. Learning methods to relax can certainly help. A job interview is likely to go better if you have less anxiety, so deep breathing and other techniques are worth a try.

However, your beliefs are even more powerful than any specific techniques. Alter your beliefs and you alter your entire approach to a situation. Have the right beliefs, and you will always be more relaxed and at ease. But how do you install these useful beliefs in your mind?

Stories and questions can help. Read the following story once or twice. See if it doesn't start to affect your thinking.

A Luck Story

A man once lost a handful of money in the wind. People walking by commented on his bad luck as he chased the bills down the street. Most of them he never found, but one dollar bill landed in front of the window to a motorcycle shop. He noticed the large new motorcycle in the window, and the sign about a raffle for it. He spent a dollar on a ticket.

The day of the drawing came and he won the new motorcycle. Everyone told him how lucky he was, but he just smiled and said, "Who knows what is good luck and what is bad?" He enjoyed the motorcycle, though, and counted his use of it among his blessings.

Then one day he had an accident on it, and broke his leg. His friends told him they felt sad for the bad luck he had. He just smiled and said, "Who knows what is good luck and what is bad?"

A war started, and many young men were drafted to

fight. Most of them died, but this man was exempted from the draft because of his broken leg. His friends pointed out how lucky he was. He smiled, of course, and said, "Who knows what is good and what is bad?"

The story could go on, but you get the point. How many times have you heard about a friend or the friend of a friend who had bad luck that turned into good luck? For example, sometimes a man is fired and as a result finds the job of his dreams, or starts a successful business.

We don't know what the future will bring. We just play the odds. If we remember that, it is difficult to sustain the stress-causing belief that a situation *must* go a certain way to be good.

Having a bad job interview, or losing some money in a bad investment, or getting lost while traveling - any of these could be the best thing that could happen to you. You just don't know.

The next time you feel tense or worried because you think something has to go a certain way, remember that guy who won the motorcycle. Question your belief that you know how things have to be. Just smile, do your best and wait to see what good things come your way.

Four Luck Exercises

1. Worrying Less

List some things you are worried about. Do it later if there is nothing worrying you now. Try several techniques to stop the worrying, and note which work best for you.

My Worry: _____

What Helped: _____

My Worry: _____

What Helped: _____

My Worry: _____

What Helped: _____

My Worry: _____

What Helped: _____

2. Relaxing

Try several relaxation techniques from the list above. Write down four that work for you. Then use them over the coming week or two, until they become habit.

What Relaxes Me: _____

What Relaxes Me: _____

What Relaxes Me: _____

What Relaxes Me: _____

3. Using Stories

Accepting and relaxing with the situation sometimes requires a change of beliefs. This can be accomplished with stories that resonate with you. Write down at least one example of a situation that seemed bad for you or someone you know, but which actually resulted in some good luck.

A Story To Remember: _____

_____

_____

_____

_____

_____

_____

4. Challenging Beliefs

Another way to relax and accept what is happening is to change specific beliefs about what "should" or "must" happen. One way to do this is to challenge those beliefs with simple questions. For example, when you feel that things are going all wrong, you could ask, "Do I really know how things need to be, or is it possible I am assuming too much?"

~ Steve Gillman ~

"Stress exists because we insist."

- Guy Finley

What ideas are you insisting on that cause you stress? Write down several. They might be as simple as "I need to get that yard work done," or "This meeting has to go well." Then challenge these ideas or beliefs.

My idea or belief: _____

A challenging question: _____

My idea or belief: _____

A challenging question: _____

My idea or belief: _____

A challenging question: _____

My idea or belief: _____

A challenging question: _____

My idea or belief: _____

A challenging question: _____

~ Secrets of Lucky People ~

Success is spending the whole afternoon relaxing on the river bank and taking in the scenery without feeling guilty about it.

- Anonymous

Chapter 15
The Dirty Mechanic

The Power Of An Open Mind

Education's purpose is to replace an empty mind with an open one.

- Malcolm Forbes

The man wasn't actually dirty, but he always looked that way. He wore old stained jeans, and his hands were permanently darkened from his work as a mechanic. When he came into the real estate office and told the receptionist that he wanted to look at some properties, some of the agents noticed him and went back to their important gossip.

They assumed that there wasn't much money to be made with this man. They followed the advice of their own prejudice and ignored him. Michael, on the other hand, walked up to the front desk and told the receptionist that he could meet with the man, even though he was busy with paperwork. He figured he might as well see what the man was looking for.

"I want to invest in fixer-uppers," the mechanic explained. Michael listened and took notes. "I haven't invested in real estate before, but here's my idea." Another agent walked by behind him and rolled his eyes at Michael. All the agents had met people who thought they knew how to get rich in real estate. Normally, they either had bad ideas or if they were good, they never followed through.

"I think there is money to be made in buying houses, fixing them up, and then leasing them out to folks who would also be given an option to buy. It makes it easier for them to get into a house without a large down payment. I think I can make a lot of money doing this if I can find the right houses."

As it turned out, the man had a fair amount of money to invest. He had been saving a good portion of the income from his car repair shop for a long time. He even had a large line of credit already arranged with a local bank.

Over the next couple years Michael sold him more than twenty houses. He almost could have made a living on just the commissions from sales to this investor. It was a lot of money, and he made it because he had an open mind.

It probably wouldn't surprise you to know that Michael became very successful over the years. In fact, he went into a partnership with the mechanic and made even more than he could have from commissions alone.

It also isn't very surprising that some of the other real estate agents were not as successful as him. Some of them didn't even survive in the profession for very long. In this true story, and in our own experiences, we can see the value of having an open mind. But what does that mean exactly?

~ Steve Gillman ~

What An Open Mind Isn't

I found the following two dictionary definitions for "open minded":

1. Receptive to new and different ideas or the opinions of others;
2. Not too narrow or conservative in one's thought, expression, or conduct.

Now, that sounds like a reasonable person, doesn't it?

To be such an open minded person means to be "receptive" then, but it doesn't mean we have to take to heart everything we receive. For example, we might be open enough to meet any person, but this doesn't mean that once we know the person we have to continue a relationship. We also don't have to entertain any worthless idea. It is one thing to listen to a new opinion, and quite another to embrace it.

I always love to read about the Amazing Randi, a magician who regularly proves psychics and others to be charlatans. For example, he has shown many audiences exactly how psychic "spoon benders" do what they do - and it isn't by using any special powers. Interestingly, no matter how many times Randi uncovers the frauds, people still want to believe that some of these guys are using telekinesis to bend those spoons or move objects.

Early in life, Randi was placed in charge of an astrology column for a newspaper in Canada. He simply cut out and shuffled up old entries and pasted them onto the various signs randomly to create each day's "astrological readings." Nonetheless, readers thought he was amazingly accurate in his understanding and advice for them.

I bring up these examples because many people think it

is simply being "open minded" to accept that people can bend spoons telekinetically, or that the "psychics" who write astrology columns are really tapping into some "higher forces." But suppose at some point we learn the real trick of "psychically" bending spoons, or read about the techniques of "cold reading" and other psychological methods used to create astrology columns and "read minds?" Then what will we think?

At this point we learn who really has an open mind. Some people will continue as "believers," but others will see that the rational explanations make more sense. The latter is the healthier, more open-minded response.

Consider another example from history: Once scientists showed that germs cause illness, anyone who continued to believe that sickness was caused by evil spirits would have been closed minded, not open minded, right? And while the effects of such false beliefs are clearer in a case like this, there are always consequences to being closed-minded.

Being open-minded then, doesn't mean believing anything and everything. It doesn't mean wasting your time seriously considering nonsense for which there is no evidence. What does it mean?

Having An Open Mind

An open minded person has an active mind, a reflective mind, and an exploring mind. She is willing to accept that there are things we don't understand, and that sometimes we have a wrong understanding of things. He is willing to take a second look at almost everything if there is a reason to (like new evidence).

Being open minded is a very common trait among lucky individuals. This makes sense in part because such a person is more likely to associate with a wider variety of people. Since other humans are the primary conduit of luck, one's "luck probability" goes up with an open mind.

It also makes one more likely to embrace new opportunities, ideas, and technologies. With an open mind, a person doesn't dismiss things as easily just because they are outside what is considered "normal." This leads to a higher probability of good fortune.

An open mind also stimulates creativity. Skepticism certainly has it's place, as I point out above. But that place is never during the process of generating creative ideas. Brainstorming experts will tell you that many bad ideas lead to good ones, and the surest way to kill the flow of new ideas is to be too critical and skeptical too early in the creative process (of course critical analysis is necessary later, before adopting ideas as goals).

Creativity means more potential opportunities, and more ways to capitalize on opportunities. Don't stifle your creativity if you want more luck in your life, and don't put too much trust in your first judgments about people. Keep an open mind.

Luck Exercise

List a few possible opportunities you've passed up due to your skepticism, and/or list some beliefs or ideas your friends have which you don't share. Then take a second look, noting (in writing) any evidence you can think of for alternate views from your own.

You don't have to change your mind about any of these things, and probably shouldn't in most cases. Just take an honest look. The point here is simply to open your mind and train it to look at things from more than one perspective.

~ Secrets of Lucky People ~

I am/was skeptical of: _____

My second look: _____

I am/was skeptical of: _____

My second look: _____

I am/was skeptical of: _____

My second look: _____

Creativity requires the courage to let go of certainties.

- Erich Fromm

Chapter 16
Sometimes Thorns Have Roses

Optimism

The optimist sees the rose and not its thorns.
The pessimist stares at the thorns, oblivious of the rose.

- Kahlil Gibran

You can see the rose and the thorns, of course. For example, Donald Trump, in his book, *How To Get Rich*, says that one should be optimistic, but he follows that by saying one should always be prepared for the worst. That "rose and the thorns" combination is what he refers to as being a "tough optimist."

A Very Short Story

Sam always had a pessimistic outlook. He believed that most things would go badly for him in the future, and he was proven correct by his experiences. Scott believed things generally would be okay in his future, and he was correct as well. Their "life results" were not unrelated to their beliefs.

~ Secrets of Lucky People ~

The bottom line is that optimism works. How motivated could you be in the pursuit of any goal if you did not allow for some possibility of success? You can quote the odds of success or failure all you want, but in the end, it is how you feel about the probabilities that determines how diligently you will pursue a goal, and therefore how likely you are to succeed.

Not surprisingly, studies show that optimistic people are more likely to be lucky people. They are also generally happier than pessimistic people. An optimistic person not only has more luck, then, but almost certainly enjoys her success more. She concentrates on the good aspects of her life.

Pessimistic people will complain even when they are successful. They might note how much better it could have been, or how hard it was to get there. You might say that they had enough luck to succeed in any case, but how lucky can "success" be if you can't enjoy it?

Of course, one could argue that a higher prevalence of good luck among optimists doesn't prove that their optimism causes their good fortune. Who knows? The research is thin. But on the other hand, if we know that there is a strong correlation between the two, and that optimists are happier anyhow, why shouldn't we try a more optimistic approach to life?

An important point about optimism: Don't be too specific. In other words, don't believe that things will turn out exactly as you want them to. This is a recipe for disillusionment and eventual bitterness, and it is unnecessary. It is enough to think and feel that things will go well for you, and that you will get what you need, even if not exactly what you wanted.

~ Steve Gillman ~

A Note To Pessimists

New to optimism? Be sure to do the exercises at the end of this chapter. They are designed to help change your mind set.

But suppose what others call your pessimism is just a realistic approach to life, at least in your mind? Do you need to believe in things regardless of evidence? Not at all. You can still generate optimistic feelings about the future without any appeal to faith, and without being unrealistic. Here are three good ways to do this.

1. Take A Historical Perspective

Think back to times in your life that were worse than now. This makes it very obvious that things can change for the better. You have good and bad times, success and failure. With that pattern in mind, you can realistically say and believe that there are better times coming, right? You can look at the historical reality and so feel different about the future.

Don't just read this explanation. Go ahead and actually do the mental exercise. Intellectualizing won't generate the feelings of optimism very effectively.

2. Notice The Good

See what goes right, both in your own life and other's lives. Note the successes you have, however small. Actually write them down if you can. Consciously bringing your attention to the positive in this way will put you in a different mental state - a more productive one.

3. See Optimism As Self Confidence

An optimistic outlook doesn't mean that you think everything will turn out okay all the time or that everything will go how you want it to. It can be a simple recognition that you can deal with whatever comes your way and make it into something good (a useful lesson if nothing else). Consider how you have survived any and all things so far, and look at how good things are for you despite past challenges.

In other words, it may help to narrow the focus of your optimism. Never mind the rest of the world for the moment. Just see that you are capable of making your own future into something good. Concentrate on your own abilities, and you will likely feel more optimistic.

Two Luck Exercises

1. Overcoming Pessimism

List a few areas of your life where you are uncertain, or even downright pessimistic about the outcome. Then list some reasons why you'll have a good outcome. You might say, for example, "Because I am going to try a new approach," or "Because I will do what it takes to make it work," or something more specific to the situation.

It is helpful to have some real reasons, meaning evidence. Without that, these affirmations won't change how you feel as effectively.

For each item, you might also want to add something like, "But even if I don't get the result I want, it will be okay because..." and then give a reason or two, such as "I'll find another way," or "there will be other opportunities," This is to keep you from stressing over a specific result, while still allowing you to feel optimistic about the future.

I'm not so sure about: _____

Why it will be okay: _____

I'm not so sure about: _____

Why it will be okay: _____

I'm not so sure about: _____

Why it will be okay: _____

I'm not so sure about: _____

Why it will be okay: _____

2. Generating More Optimism

Here is an easy and effective exercise. Simply list five or ten things about which you are optimistic. These can be a mix of personal plans and "state of the world" things if you like. The process can put you in a good mood and make you feel more motivated. Do this enough, and focusing on the good things that are likely to happen will become a habit that helps you generate more good luck.

1. _____

~ Secrets of Lucky People ~

2._____

3._____

4._____

5._____

6._____

7._____

8._____

9._____

10._____

Optimist: A man who gets treed by a lion but enjoys the scenery.

- Walter Winchell

Chapter 17
My Lucky Flat Tire

Useful Beliefs

Believe and act as if it were impossible to fail.

- Charles F. Kettering

Do superstitions lead to better luck? That has yet to be answered scientifically (my guess is no). What has been discovered, is that lucky and unlucky people believe in different superstitions. A few years ago 400 people took part in an online survey dealing with the psychology of superstition and luck.

First, participants were asked if they were lucky or unlucky. Then they were asked about a number of superstitious behaviors.

There were clear differences in responses between the self-described lucky and unlucky people.

Lucky people engaged in superstitious behaviors that were meant to bring about good results. They carried lucky charms, knocked on wood, and crossed their fingers more often. For example, 49% of them crossed their fingers for luck, as opposed to just 30% of unlucky people. On the other hand, they were less likely to believe in superstitions about bad luck.

Unlucky people were much more likely to believe in superstitions about bad luck. They believed walking under a ladder or breaking a mirror meant bad luck. They were afraid of the number 13. In fact 55% of unlucky people feared the number 13, as opposed to just 22% of lucky people.

Essentially the study found that lucky people engage in superstitious activities that make them feel good, while unlucky people's superstitions make them fear the worst. These obviously can be self-fulfilling prophecies. In other words, people can make their own luck - good or bad.

Useful Lies

I certainly don't think that such nonsense beliefs are necessary. On the other hand, if wearing a lucky hat makes a mountain climber feel more comfortable, maybe he shouldn't fight his feeling. I am decidedly not superstitious myself, but I think many superstitions fall into the category of "useful beliefs," or "useful lies."

What I call useful lies are not necessarily lies, but are beliefs which benefit us, even though they cannot be proven, and often seem contrary to common sense. Their truth or falsity is mostly irrelevant in regards to their usefulness. The important thing is whether they do more good than harm.

They don't even need to be believed in the traditional sense. In fact, I prefer to call them "operating principles," rather than beliefs. I sometimes refer to them as lies because we essentially pretend to believe what we have insufficient evidence for. Here is an example from my own life.

~ Steve Gillman ~

How To Use A Lie - My Flat Tire Story

A couple summers back, I was on Highway 50 at 4:30 one morning, heading out of Canon City to climb Mount Yale. The trail head is about two hours away, and it's important to start early, in order to summit and start down before the afternoon thunderstorms move in.

A little after five, as I was approaching Salida, I saw a scattering of rocks on the road. They had fallen during the night, and it was too late to avoid them. The front tire on the drivers side was punctured by a rock and almost immediately lost its air. I pulled off on the side of the highway.

I opened the trunk, and the first thing I noticed was that everything was wet. Somehow the trunk had been leaking when it rained. Next, I saw that the bolt holding the jack in place was rusted because of the moisture. I tried turning the nut. No luck. I took the crowbar and pounded on it. Nothing.

At this point I decided that this was a test of my ingenuity. It was a chance to use my creative problem solving skills. I could have fun with this.

I moved everything out of the trunk, so I could get at the spare tire under the carpet. The wing-nut holding this was rusted solidly in place just like the nut for the jack, and couldn't be pounded free with the crowbar. I tried using a rock, managing to crush my finger. This was my opportunity to dance around, and practice my profanity.

Then I remembered that in a box in the trunk there was a small hacksaw, with a blade about four inches long. Kicking at the jack had only bent the metal brackets, so I decided to saw through the bolt. Halfway through, the saw broke. Fortunately, I was able to fix it, and I eventually cut the bolt.

The jack didn't work. It was too rusted up. I found a

~ Secrets of Lucky People ~

quart of oil in the trunk and dripped some on the threads of the jack, then pounded on it with the crowbar. It finally moved, and I was able to use it.

I washed up in the river, enjoyed the rising sun, and then started sawing through the much thicker bolt holding the spare tire in place. The saw broke. I fixed it, and then it jammed. I started over. Eventually the tire was free. Ten minutes after that I had the flat tire off, and the spare put on.

Then I heard a hissing sound. The tire I had just put on was leaking air. Fortunately I had a bicycle tire pump with me, so I used that to inflate it. After more than two hours, I was on the road again.

It was seven when I arrived at the tire shop in Salida and discovered that it opened at eight. I waited. The tire was beyond repair, so I had a new tire put on.

By now it was too late to go climb the mountain. It was also raining - an awful day to be up high on a rocky peak. I would have been wet and cold, or possibly worse, had it not been for the accident. Maybe that flat tire was meant to happen.

Do I believe that? No, not at all. I don't have to believe that everything happens for a reason. It is useful enough to act as if life works that way. I could have been angry, discouraged, or in an otherwise unproductive state. Instead I acted as though things happen for a reason.

What does this do? It gets you thinking about the good that comes from a "bad" situation. At times I was having fun trying to figure out how to change that tire. It meant I avoided a cold wet hike. I came home and I wrote this story up into a page for one of my web sites, and got a lot of other work done.

(And now I have used the experience as an illustrative lesson in this book, squeezing even more value out of that flat tire. I also went back another day and climbed Mount Yale in much nicer weather.)

In other words, I made a good thing out of a bad thing. In terms of how I felt, it was my lucky day. That is what useful lies can do for you.

More Useful Beliefs

You can have anything you want if you will give up the belief that you can't have it.

- Dr. Robert Anthony

I would say that the quote above is almost certainly false, or impossible to prove at best, and yet perhaps inspiring nonetheless. In other words, it could be a useful belief if you don't take it too far. Here are some more "operating principles" or beliefs that you may want to use for better luck and success in life.

- There is no failure if I choose to learn something from each experience.
- There is always a way to make something good out of everything that happens.
- A delay is not a denial.
- I can choose a better way to do anything.
- The future is not a projection of the past, but a result of choices I make right now.
- What I do not know I can learn.
- If others have done something, I can learn how to do it too.
- I have powers that I've only begun to tap into.
- I can always find a way to get where I want to go.

~ Secrets of Lucky People ~

Remember, the crucial point isn't whether you can instantly make yourself believe these things, or even that you should (you may have noticed that I am not a big fan of any absolute beliefs). If it helps, you can reinforce them in your mind by looking for evidence to support them. But on the other hand, it may be enough to simply act as though they are true, and to look at circumstances from the viewpoint they create.

Luck Exercise

List a few useful beliefs or "operating principles" that you can use to approach situations from a more productive state of mind. As you go through your week, list any examples of how a particular belief helped you. The first two are provided for you, and are universal enough for anyone to use.

My useful belief: Everything happens for a reason.

How I used it: _____

My useful belief: There is something good in every bad situation.

How I used it: _____

My useful belief: _____

How I used it: _____

~ Steve Gillman ~

My useful belief: _____

How I used it: _____

My useful belief: _____

How I used it: _____

Everything can be taken from a man but ... the last of the human freedoms - to choose one's attitude in any given set of circumstances, to choose one's own way.

- Victor Frankl

Chapter 18
Gorillas And Lottery Tickets

Creativity And Non-Conformity

*Two roads diverged in a wood,
and I - I took the one less traveled by,
and that has made all the difference.*

- Robert Frost

There is some evidence that more creativity results in more of what many would call luck. No real surprise here - more creative and new ideas obviously means more opportunities for good or "lucky" ideas to come about. But how do you become more creative?

There are actually many techniques for generating ideas. Books on problem solving, for example, are full of these techniques. You can use them in a given situation for immediate results, or train yourself to use them habitually for a permanently more creative mind.

However, there is one important aspect that this lesson addresses. It is the tendency we have to conform, and how this stifles our creativity. Learn when and how to step outside the lines, and you will be far more creative, and therefore potentially luckier in life.

Conformity To The "Rules"

In 1999 Daniel Simons, from the University of Illinois, published a paper with C.F. Chabris, in the journal *Perception and Psychophysics*. It was titled; *Gorillas in Our Midst: Sustained Inattentional Blindness for Dynamic Events*. It reported a simple experiment in which subjects watched a 30-second film of people playing basketball, to see if they noticed a man in the gorilla suit on the court.

Richard Wiseman, the expert on luck and creativity, took the idea and ran with it. He showed a similar film to many groups of people. In it, three basketball players are dressed in white t-shirts, and three in black. They are playing a game, but in the middle of the film, a man in a gorilla suit walks into the center of the court and beats his chest for the camera. This is something very obvious, which most viewers would notice, right?

However, viewers had been instructed to watch for and count the number of passes made by one team. Because they were focusing on that task, when they were later asked for their totals, and then asked if they noticed anything unusual in the film, only a small percentage ever said yes. In fact, when Wiseman introduced more competitiveness to the process (for example, by pitting one side of the room against the other in a test of accuracy), the number of people who noticed the gorilla was as low as 5%.

This is an example of how "in the box" we can be when we're in a given situation. We stay within the normal "rules" and we do what everyone else is doing. It can be a useful part of our psychology, both because of the social cohesiveness that results and because too much awareness of everything else going on can interfere with concentrating

~ Secrets of Lucky People ~

on the task at hand.

However, there are times when the task at hand should be to think outside of that box, to do what others are not doing, and to see something new.

Thinking Outside Of The Box

The "box" is the normal way of doing things and looking at things. It is the assumptions that almost everyone involved is making. The best way to start thinking out of the box then, is to identify and challenge all the common assumptions that make up thinking inside the box.

For example, one of the major liquor brands was faltering years ago, and they couldn't seem to boost their sales. Promotions, lowering the price, getting better shelf placement - these were the "in the box" solutions. Then someone challenged the common assumptions, by asking "What if we stopped the promotions and just raised the price?"

The price was raised as an experiment, and sales soon doubled. As it turns out, some types of liquor are bought quite often as gifts. Buyers don't want to buy the most expensive one, but they also don't want to seem cheap, so they won't buy products which don't cost enough. Now consider what happens to your profit margins when you raise the price and double the sales. That's the power of thinking outside of the box.

Ways To Get Outside Of The Box

It is better to have enough ideas for some of them to be wrong, than to be always right by having no ideas at all.

- Edward DeBono

Imagine walking in and seeing those people viewing the basketball film with the gorilla. Your eyes would likely follow theirs to the screen, but you would notice the gorilla, and wonder why they didn't. Why? Because you would not know the "rules" of what they were doing until they were explained to you, nor feel constrained by them until you were actually participating.

In other words, you would still be an "outsider." This suggests that an "outsider perspective" is one way to get your thinking out of the box. Mentally step away from what is going on and see it as a complete stranger would. That's one way to see something new. Let's look at some others.

Challenge Assumptions

This is a great creative problem solving technique, as well as a powerful way to generate new ideas. The difficult part is to identify the assumptions. If you are designing a new motorcycle, for example, you need to write down assumptions like "speed matters," "it has to run on gas" and "it needs two wheels." This is not because you expect to prove these wrong, but because challenging them can lead to creative possibilities. Maybe the time has come for an electric three-wheeled motorcycle (maybe there is one already).

Assume The Absurd

Another way to get to creative non-conforming ideas is to do a little exercise called "assume the absurd." This can be either fun or annoying, depending on how open-minded you are. Essentially, you just start making absurd assumptions, and then find ways to make sense of them. The easiest way to do this is by asking "what if" questions.

~ Secrets of Lucky People ~

What if a carpet cleaning business was better off with half as many customers? It seems absurd, but work with it. Hmm...less stressful, perhaps. More profitable if each customer was worth three times as much. Is that possible? Commercial jobs have large easy-to-clean spaces (theaters, offices), generate much more revenue per hour than houses do, and with fewer headaches. Focusing on getting those accounts could be the most profitable way to go - not so absurd.

Get Out

Another way to have more innovative ideas is to literally do your thinking out of the box. Get out of the house or the office. Park the car and walk around. New environments can stimulate new ideas.

Adapt Foreign Ideas

Always look around at how others outside of your usual "circle" of friends and associates are doing things. For example, on busses in many parts of the world, salesmen put a product into everyone's hands and let them hold it while they do a sales pitch. Then you have to give back "your" product or pay for it. It's very effective.

How could you use the principle in a business?

Do Things Differently

There was an experiment in creativity in which brainstorming sessions were done in two ways. The first set consisted of the normal procedures, with people producing ideas and a moderator writing them down. In the second set of sessions, one simple change was made. The participants were told to take their shoes off.

Consistently, people produced more ideas when their shoes were off. This is a neat little example of how just getting out of our normal routines and social conventions can stimulate more creative thought.

Social Conformity

The non-conformist club decided on a uniform for its members, but couldn't get them to wear it.

- Anonymous

As noted, one of the things that stifles our creativity is our need to conform to the people around us. We tend to do what they're doing and think what they're thinking. There are certain expectations which are there, even if we aren't always aware of them.

Of course there is good reason to conform most of the time. Singing while in a bookstore, refusing to shake hands, or certain other demonstrations of non-conformity probably won't give you any creative edge in life. We follow most unspoken social "rules" because they benefit all of us.

On the other hand, there are times when breaking the rules or not following the herd makes sense. If everyone goes to the closest check-out registers at the grocery store, you might get through faster by going to one further down. If most people are using credit cards and as a result are in financial trouble, you might do well to be a non-conformist and pay cash.

Luck or opportunity is often where the crowd isn't. For example, many tourists here in Colorado like to pan for gold. Of course, they all go to the same easily-accessible

~ Secrets of Lucky People ~

places, so these places don't have much gold left. Where would you have more luck looking for gold? Wherever the people don't go, of course.

When I was sixteen I hitchhiked across the country. This was back when hitchhiking was common. I came to one freeway entrance ramp and saw over 20 hitchhikers lined up with their thumbs out. As I walked past them I heard complaints about how long they had been waiting.

I just kept walking. A mile later, away from the crowd, there was room for a driver to pull over, and he didn't have to make a choice about who to pick up. I easily got a ride there - my reward for being a non-conformist.

Non-Conformity - The Lottery Example

Here's an example of how being a non-conformist can even increase your luck in the lottery. It is very common for people to bet on numbers that represent birthdays, which means the numbers below 32, since there are no more than 31 days in any month. Since so many people do this, when they win they usually split the pot, sometimes among several winners. This means that each winner gets less money.

On the other hand, when the winning numbers are all over 32, less tickets have those numbers. This means that the money is split fewer ways and each winning ticket is worth more. In fact, in these cases it is more common for one winner to get the whole prize. All numbers are equally likely to come up, so if you bet the ones between 32 and 40, you actually have a better chance to win more money.

This doesn't make the lottery a good bet, by the way. It just makes it a better bet. But it is also a great little example of how getting away from the crowd can be a creative way to improve your luck.

~ Steve Gillman ~

Luck Exercise

This exercise is meant to train your mind to look for more creative and non-conformist solutions. List some of the ways people normally do things, and then find different but still useful alternatives.

The usual way it is done: _____

A different way: _____

The usual way it is done: _____

A different way: _____

The usual way it is done: _____

A different way: _____

The usual way it is done: _____

A different way: _____

The usual way it is done: _____

A different way: _____

The usual way it is done: _____

~ Secrets of Lucky People ~

A different way: _____

> *If past history was all there was to the game, the richest people would be librarians.*
>
> *- Warren Buffett*

Chapter 19
How To Buy An Island For A 94% Discount

Ask And You Might Receive

Ask, and it shall be given you; seek, and ye shall find; knock, and it shall be opened unto you.

- Jesus

Asking for things you want is a sure way to have better luck. It is an obvious lesson, right? But then how many of us would have done what Richard Branson did in the following story (this was before he was a billionaire).

Richard Branson and his wife were in the Virgin Islands, looking at small islands for sale. They had no intention of buying one, but their trip was paid for by the real estate company as long as they were looking. It was a way to get a vacation when they were short on cash.

One particular island caught their imaginations, however. It was lush and green, with a lake, and a nice beach. Branson decided that he did want an island after all. He asked about the price, and was told it was three million pounds. He offered 150,000 pounds. The agent repeated

~ Secrets of Lucky People ~

the asking price, and Branson said he would pay 200,000 pounds, and no more.

With that, the vacation was over. In fact, their things were abruptly put outside of the hotel room. Offering 93% less than the asking price apparently offended the agent. However, the story didn't end there.

Later, back in England, Branson found the owner. The man had never even been to the island, and he was very anxious to sell it. Branson offered him 175,000 pounds. The offer was rejected. That still is not the end of the story, however.

Several months later Branson received a call from the owner. He said he would take 180,000 pounds for it. Branson found a way to borrow the money, and he closed the deal. He bought the island for just 6% of the asking price, and 20,000 pounds less than one of his previous offers.

This is the kind of reward you can get for asking. Perhaps at some point someone even thought they would pay 300,000 pounds for the island, but didn't want to "insult" the owner with such a low offer. You might look like a fool for asking for a 90% discount, right?

But then again, Branson got it even cheaper. Maybe looking like a fool is a risk worth taking for a deal like that. You never know until you ask.

Advertising

Sometimes "asking" can be as simple as advertising your needs. Many years ago I bought my first house by putting an ad in the newspaper. I said I wanted something that the owner would finance with just a small down payment. That is exactly what I got (although I ended up with better financing from a bank). One phone call was all it took.

When I say advertising, I mean literally and metaphorically. Placing an ad in the newspaper classified section, or online can work for all sorts of things. Of course, "advertising" can also be simply talking about what you want. This is how people can know what you want, and so be able to help you.

In that first house I had an almost-new couch I paid just $35 for. I simply mentioned to the neighbor that I was looking for one. His wife had just recently decided that she didn't like the color of their three-month-old couch, and wanted to get rid of it for 10% of what she paid. Lucky me.

Another example: I was recently playing the board game, "Cash Flow," at a local real estate office. The game I really like to play is chess, so I asked the others there if they knew anyone who played chess (I advertised). One said, "Someone else asked me the same thing yesterday." As it turned out, it was the vice-president of a local bank - a good person to know if we need a loan someday (and a good friendship developed as well).

Remember the secret of the guy who got all the dates in Lesson One? He just asked a lot of woman out. Of course most said no, but some said yes. This, by the way, also demonstrates why I call this lesson "Ask And You Might Receive." It doesn't guarantee the results you want in a particular situation. It just puts the odds more in your favor. Ask for enough things and you'll get some of them, and certainly more than if you remain silent.

There is an exception to this rule of telling everyone what you want. Don't do it when what you want is a long-term goal and the people you tell are critical or discouraging. They don't need to know if you want to become a wealthy writer or a movie star. These kinds of goals should generally only be shared with those who are encouraging and positive in their comments.

~ Secrets of Lucky People ~

More On Why Asking Makes You Luckier

Even when you don't get what you are asking for, the process itself generates opportunities. People like to help others, so you are making them feel good when you ask for help, and we all like to be around those who make us feel good. In other words, you're improving a relationship (as long as you're not too demanding too often), which can bring luck your way in other matters in the future. Plus, more interaction with others generally means more possibilities of all sorts.

Luck Exercise

List some things that you would like to have, or some things that you would like to happen in your life. One by one, make a point to mention these desires to at least one or two people. Put a big check mark next to each item as you do so.

To really improve your luck, do this exercise until you find that you are automatically advertising your desires to the world.

I would like: _____

I would like: _____

I would like: _____

I would like: _____

I would like: _____

~ Steve Gillman ~

I would like: _____

I would like: _____

Asking increases the odds of receiving.

- Steven Scott

Chapter 20
The Illiterate Millionaire

Using Your Personal Assets

Do what you can, with what you have, where you are.

- Theodore Roosevelt

Do you sometimes wonder if you have what you need to achieve your goals? Maybe you need more money, more education, or more help. Lucky people simply start anyhow, and use whatever they have at the moment. You can learn as you go, and get what you need along the way.

A True Story

Mark Nabors (not his real name) didn't have any money to start his business. What did he do? He used what he had - his ideas, his experience in the industry, and the people he knew. He convinced a former employer to rent him some equipment to start a machine shop. They agreed that he would start paying the rental fees once he had made some money. He called people he knew and found some customers. This was the beginning of his machine and tool company in Nevada.

Today Mark's company makes millions of dollars per year. He did it despite not having money or business experience. Mark is working with a tutor these days as well, because there is one more thing that he didn't have when he started his business: The ability to read and write.

Remember that the next time you think that "lucky" people have big advantages which you don't have. Start where you are and use what you have. It is what everyone has to do in any case, right?

What Do You Have?

You may have little in the way of money or physical assets, but all of us have many valuable things we can use to create a better life. These "things" might be good character traits, or skills. Even simple advantages like having access to a decent library can be a great help in pursuing one's goals.

It is also good to remember that little things can mean a lot over time. Are you like many people who spend $3 on coffee every work day? Believe it or not, if you were to quit the coffee, and put that $15 per week into an tax-free retirement account that grew at 8% annually, you would have almost $300,000 in 40 years.

Maybe you have a little time. That can be valuable. If you drive 25 minutes to your job, you have over 200 hours per year to learn something useful that would advance you towards your goals. Most public libraries have hundreds of books on tapes or CDs, and they are free to use.

What else might you have? Some suggestions follow. How can each of these be used to move you towards your goals?

~ Secrets of Lucky People ~

- A Job
- A Car
- Good Work Habits
- Good Rapport With Others
- A Great Smile
- A Quick Mind
- A Creative Mind
- Physical Strength
- A College Degree
- Books
- A Bicycle
- Family
- Good Friends
- Various Acquaintances
- A Computer
- A Hobby
- A House
- A Savings Account
- A Garage
- A Telephone
- Certain Skills
- Certain Knowledge

What other assets do you have? You have your mind. Use that well, and it can lead you to everything else you need.

Luck Exercise

List what you have that might help you towards your goals or dreams. Include character traits, money, skills, friends, and anything else of value. Then make a note or two about how you might use each asset.

You'll have to do this exercise several times to get the

most benefit from it, because you will not initially think of some things as having value for achieving your goals. A pen, for example, can be very valuable, if you use it to write out a plan that gets you where you want to be.

I have: _____

How I can use it: _____

I have: _____

How I can use it: _____

I have: _____

How I can use it: _____

I have: _____

How I can use it: _____

I have: _____

How I can use it: _____

I have: _____

How I can use it: _____

~ Secrets of Lucky People ~

I have: _____

How I can use it: _____

You are the only one who can use your ability.
It is an awesome responsibility.

- Zig Ziglar

Chapter 21
The Lazy Investor

Priorities

Action expresses priorities.

- Mahatma Gandhi

Max (not his real name) worked about thirty hours a week as a real estate agent and investor. He was usually very relaxed in his approach to things. He didn't really like showing houses to people, so he concentrated on buying, fixing up, and selling homes. He never lifted a hammer or a paint brush, though, preferring to pay to have all the work done.

I met him when I first started selling real estate. The first year I knew him he fixed and sold 14 houses. They were lower-priced homes, and there were always surprises, so the average profit was less than the minimum $10,000 he wanted to make on each house. He also had a partner who put up the money, so he had to split the profit. As a result he made just $50,000 or so that year.

However, this was many years ago, back when $50,000 was worth a lot more than now. Also, this money was in addition to the commissions he made as a real estate agent. A lot of people thought he was pretty lucky. They wondered how he could do this while working so few hours.

Having worked with him on a couple deals, I can tell you an important part of his success: He knew how to prioritize. The most important elements of the process were finding houses, seeing what they needed, figuring the cost, determining what the house would sell for when done, and then making an offer that left room for a large profit. These were the actions Max concentrated on.

He could have made more money on a given house, if he did some of the painting himself. He could have micromanaged everything to keep the costs down a bit. He could have done a lot of things differently. But then he would have less time to find the next house.

He had identified the elements of the process that were most important. They can be summed up as "finding and arranging the deals." This was his priority, and as long as he concentrated on this, he only needed to work 30 hours per week.

Prioritizing

Don't tell me where your priorities are. Show me where you spend your money and I'll tell you what they are.

- James W. Frick

To the quote above, I would add "Show me where you spend your time." There is little research in this area, but my own observation is that those who are considered lucky know how to prioritize better than unlucky people. This is just common sense when it comes to success in life. If you do the important things first, and you do the *most* important things more often, you'll have better results.

This certainly isn't just about financial success. One of the reasons that Max didn't work more is that his family life was very important to him. He set his priorities according to his values. That is part of what made him so lucky. This is the "big picture" view of prioritizing. You need to discover your values and arrange your time accordingly.

However, even once you prioritize on the large matters, don't forget the details. Suppose, for example, that you decided to set aside time to start a writing career, but you find that you're rearranging the desk too often, or reading too many writer's magazines. The priority should probably be writing something every day in this case. But we often forget what elements are most important, and it's easy to justify all the things that waste our time.

It's not surprising that we find it difficult to properly prioritize. We have potentially conflicting interests, after all. We may want to grow a business, spend time with family, and just relax and watch TV. So how do we decide where to allocate your time and when?

The simple answer is that we do our best and try to be honest with ourselves. Some lucky people probably have a more innate sense of what is important and when. However, experience tells us that we can learn to think differently - more like them perhaps - and so get better results.

One way to do this is to actually make decisions openly and consciously. Often we do things from habit or unconscious motives. Bring it out in the open, and it is easier to see if it is the right choice. If you are going to sit in front of that TV for five hours, for example, ask yourself, "Is five hours of television a priority to me according to my values?"

Chances are, you can't answer yes honestly, and the question itself will motivate you to find a better use of your time. On the other hand, if you are sick, maybe you do need that time in front of the TV. The point is not to deny yourself a pleasure, but to be sure that you get real value from what you do, according to standards which you choose for yourself.

I sometimes find myself cleaning up my desk too often. If I ask myself about it, I can't honestly say that it's important to the business. I can see it's an excuse to avoid whatever I need to be doing at the moment. But I have to consciously stop and look at my actions from time to time, because they continue without much consciousness if I let them.

Be more conscious of your true priorities.

How To Prioritize Your Way To A Luckier Life

Here is a five-step plan for better prioritization.

1. Identify what you truly value.

You'll always have several important values, so recognize the natural hierarchy of these when making your choices. Is your work, or your hobby more important? Is having big cars and boats or having financial security more valuable to you?

2. Create goals for each of your values.

If traveling the world is important, set specific goals for trips. If financial freedom is valuable, set targets for creating assets and income outside of your job. Look for goals that come naturally from your values. If you desire peace of mind, for example, don't assume that money will bring that to you; make it a goal to learn what will.

3. **Determine the most effective actions.**

What will work best for reaching those goals? Sometimes it's difficult to know this. If it is a common goal, see what has worked best for others. Otherwise, try things and see what results you get.

4. **Put those actions at the top of your "to do" list.**

If your goal is to be a famous painter, for example, you might decide you need to start each morning by getting in front of that canvas. Put that at the top of your list for the day. If you want a new boat, and need to put some money aside each week, add that to the top of Friday's list (or whatever day is payday).

5. **Repeatedly start with those highest priority items.**

Priority means "Something afforded or deserving prior attention." In other words, perhaps you should even take your morning shower *after* you work on your top priorities (if this is practical). As much as possible, put valuable tasks ahead of the less valuable. Consciously do this until it becomes a habit to think of - and do - the most effective and productive actions first.

Luck Exercise

List some important values, followed by a goal in line with that value. Then list some of the most effective actions you can take. If possible, for each goal have at least one action which you can take tomorrow morning.

~ Secrets of Lucky People ~

Value: _____

Goal: _____

Top priority actions: _____

Value: _____

Goal: _____

Top priority actions: _____

Value: _____

Goal: _____

Top priority actions: _____

Value: _____

Goal: _____

Top priority actions: _____

Value: _____

Goal: _____

Top priority actions: _____

~ Steve Gillman ~

You must see your goals clearly and specifically before you can set out for them. Hold them in your mind until they become second nature.

- Les Brown

Chapter 22
Your Plane Crash Survival Story

Control And Go With The Flow

He who controls others may be powerful, but he who has mastered himself is mightier still.

- Lao Tzu

Suppose you are lost in the wilderness with several other people after a plane crash. Some of them think you should all stay where you are until a rescue party comes.

You, however, think that the plane was so far off-course that the rescue parties are unlikely to look here. The fact that none have appeared since the plane crashed three days earlier has convinced you of this. What can you do? Let's look at four possible scenarios.

1. Do Nothing But Complain

You could just sit and let the others vote on your future - let them make the decisions for you. Then, as you wait to see what happens, you could complain and be bitter about their "stupidity." This is what many unlucky people would do.

2. Get Angry and Manipulative

You could explain why the searchers aren't likely to find you here, and then get angry when the others don't agree. You could try to manipulate some of them into taking your side, and fight for control of the group. In this case, your own desire and desperation to control the situation might turn the others away from you.

3. Do Your Best

You could just do your best to persuade others to go with you for help. After all, if you are right about the search parties not looking here, this could save everyone's life. You could go alone then if you had to, or with whoever you can convince.

4. Control What You Can

If none are persuaded, you might decide that you are safer staying with everyone else than going off by yourself. In that case you could immediately start to look for ways to survive while you wait. Start gathering fire wood and making weapons if animals are a problem. Look for shelter, food, and a source of water.

Do you notice the differences here? In the first example you whine about the situation after the decision is made, which is just a way of excusing your inaction. In the second, you try to control people's minds with anger and manipulation, which will just frustrate you.

In the third and fourth examples, you accept that you

can't control everything about the situation. Then you take control of what you can: your own mind, words and actions.

What Kind Of Control?

Anything you have to control controls you.

- Guy Finley

The above quote points to something that is difficult for most people to understand. If you feel that you must have a certain outcome, then you are forced by your own ideas to serve that image in your mind, doing whatever it takes to try to create it, even things which are destructive of your true values. You also are bound to be disappointed by any reality which is different than the one you imagine "should" exist.

Consider the story above. If you insisted on controlling the situation and the people, and thought that you "must" get a group to agree with you and go looking for help, what might happen? You could spend valuable time that is needed for survival tasks running around trying to show people how stupid they are for not agreeing with you. You might even break down the social cohesiveness that is needed for survival.

Without a doubt, if you do not succeed, you will feel miserable and demotivated. Even if you partially succeed, you may get only half-hearted help from those who are not really committed to your plan. None of this is helpful.

Notice, though, that the problem is not in trying to show the others the truth you see. Going for help may really be a good idea. The problem arises when you insist it's the only outcome you'll accept. If the others don't agree, then you are left fighting reality. Guess what? Reality usually wins.

Bill's Favorite Restaurant

There are many good restaurants around, but one, *Obsession*, is Bill's favorite. Friends were visiting from out of town, and he felt he "must" take them there. But unfortunately, when they arrived at the restaurant, there was a two-hour line to get in. "Damn" he muttered quietly. His blood pressure started to rise.

Bill's friends told him they were fine with any restaurant, but he insisted that this was the best. He had wanted to take them here for a long time. Being polite, they got in line. An hour later it was raining lightly, and everyone was cold, but they were almost inside the door, so they kept waiting. Another hour later, they were finally seated.

The table was dirty, and it took ten more minutes just for the waiter to arrive. Bill almost yelled at him, while his friends tried to make light conversation to diffuse the tension. After another long wait, everyone got a mediocre meal.

Because the dinner was so late, they decided to cancel their plans go out for drinks afterwards. Bill said his goodbyes and sullenly went home, blaming the restaurant for his mood. It seemed that the world just wouldn't cooperate with his plans.

Alternate Version:

Upon seeing the line at his favorite restaurant, Bill pulled out a piece of paper. On it he had written the names and addresses of two restaurants he had never been to before. One had Italian food, and the other Nepalese. He asked his friends, and they decided it would be fun to have Nepalese food, since none of them had tried that.

The place was unfortunately closed for renovations

when they arrived. Bill shrugged his shoulders and said, "Oh well." Too hungry to go further, he suggested a Lebanese restaurant a couple doors over. They served delicious falafel and stuffed grape leaves, he had heard.

The food was excellent, as was the conversation. His friends loved the restaurant, which was now Bill's favorite. Afterwards they walked downtown and found a great little piano bar, where they had drinks and enjoyed the music. Everyone had a great time.

Lucky People

Lucky people tend to make their own luck. Paradoxically, they are also less likely to have a need to control. In other words, they control what they can, but are also able to go with the flow when needed, as in the story above.

As pointed out in previous lessons, such people are generally more relaxed. This is partly because they don't insist that things need to go a certain way. They're more willing to think outside of the box, which sometimes can mean letting go of control, or letting go of the ways in which they normally operate and are familiar with.

This isn't a passive approach, however. You don't have to just sit there when there is something productive to do. You can step back, look around at the options and take action. But the key to this happy attitude is to not develop a strong attachment to an imagined outcome. Control what you can, and make the best of the results you get.

Lets take a look at what you can and can't control:

What You Can Control

- The words you say to others.

- The words you say to yourself (with practice).
- Your actions right now.
- Your "higher thoughts" that lead to better actions (with practice).
- Some aspects of the situation around you right now.

What You Can't Control

- Most of what others think about you - or anything else they think.
- Most of what others decide to do.
- Random unforeseeable accidents and disasters.
- The laws of nature, including those that determine the weather.
- What has happened prior to this moment.

The next time you find yourself insisting on fighting what is happening, stop and see what elements of the situation belong to which list above. Then stop going to war with what you can't control. Do what you can, and go with the flow.

Luck Exercise

Write a quick description of a situation you're facing which seems a bit out of your control. Then list several things you truly can't control about it, followed by several things which you can.

There are always some things within your control, even if only your choice to learn from a situation, or how you choose to look at it.

The situation: _____

~ Secrets of Lucky People ~

What is out of my control: _____

What I can control: _____

God, grant me the serenity
To accept the things I cannot change,
The courage to change the things I can,
And the wisdom to know the difference.

- The Serenity Prayer

Chapter 23
Ronald Reagan's Secret

Delegate

Surround yourself with the best people you can find, delegate authority, and don't interfere.

- Ronald Reagan

Ronald Reagan did many things while he was President of the United States. You can argue about whether he should have done some of the things he did, but he accomplished a lot. How was this possible while also taking many vacations and often sleeping for hours in the oval office each afternoon? Like many lucky people, he knew how to delegate.

Remember Max, the "lazy" real estate investor from the chapter on prioritizing? Apart from knowing how to prioritize, another reason he was able to succeed working just 30 hours per week was that he knew how to delegate. As mentioned, he never worked on a house himself. Contractors did that. He also had "bird dogs" finding properties for him, and other agents often handled the sales. Max just did what he was best at: making offers on profitable properties.

~ Secrets of Lucky People ~

One of the reasons that many small businesses never grow beyond a certain level is because the owners don't want to give up some control of the day-to-day tasks. They don't want to delegate properly. Consider a pizzeria owner. Could he simultaneously be the head pizza maker, delivery person and still have the time and energy to start new pizza restaurants in new locations? Not likely.

Delegation In Personal Life

I have a secret to tell. My wife and I are very frugal at times. Okay, this is no secret to our friends, and we used to live on a fairly tight budget. But despite making more money now, out of habit we still tear paper napkins in half to make them go further.

Naturally then, our friends are surprised when they learn that we "cheapskates" pay for house cleaning, and to have the lawn mowed. But it make perfect sense to us. Many of them make money to buy better TVs and other toys. We want to be able to hike, write poetry or stories, go to the local hot springs, or do something new with the business. In other words, we use money to buy time.

Also, at some level of income it becomes wasteful to do the deep cleaning if we don't enjoy it. For example, if I work on a web site for four hours while someone else cleans the house, I might make $120 for my effort and pay $40 for the cleaning. It would be counter-productive for me or my wife to scrub the cupboards.

It is also important to delegate when expertise is needed - not an easy lesson for me to learn. I always created time in other ways, as I'll explain below. But I hesitated to pay for good help. For example, we had our business for over two years before we paid to have our taxes done. Big mistake. Our tax preparer found deductions I didn't know about that saved us perhaps a thousand dollars that year alone. I wonder about how much we may have overpaid before. And delegating the hard work to him has meant no more days of frustration with confusing tax forms.

Productive Leisure Time

How does delegating make a person luckier? Having an afternoon off for a drive in the mountains because of time freed up by paying for house cleaning certainly makes me and my wife feel fortunate. But there is another important principle here. It is the principle of productive leisure time.

Many years ago, I noticed that most of my friends never had much time. They worked too much, and with all their busyness, they couldn't take advantage of opportunities like I could. I never liked jobs much, nor even most businesses, so I didn't always have one. As a result I had time. I traveled, dabbled in a few hobby/businesses, and read a lot.

How was I able to do this? I certainly didn't have much income. In fact, for much of my life every one of my friends made more money than I. But I rented rooms out, and paid off the mortgage early, so my home was a free place to live - and provided a little income even after paying all the bills. I found every way there is to do things less expensively. In fact, I once traveled for a month to South America for $1040 including airfare, hotels and everything else.

The real secret is that I had what I call productive leisure time. I could relax and think about how to save money. I had time to go to an auction (they're fun, by the way) to save $2,000 on a decent car. Other people put in a lot of hours at a job to pay the $2,000 extra for similar cars.

I had time to figure out how to do the things I wanted without much money, like when I went dog sledding in the

~ Secrets of Lucky People ~

Canadian wilderness, or cave exploring in Tennessee by volunteering to chaperone a youth group. I had time to carve and sell walking sticks, buy and sell cars, and to find a dozen other interesting ways to make some money.

You need a certain amount of productive leisure time to be really lucky. This is time to think, but also time to explore life just to see what is enjoyable for you. It is time to pursue your interests and perhaps discover a way to make those interests into an income. And though money helps a lot if you want to take advantage of opportunities, time is perhaps more important.

Buying Time

How do you arrange for more productive leisure time? One way is to buy it with smart delegation. Let's look at a couple examples.

Alex

Alex makes $14 per hour, or $21 per hour when he works overtime. He can generally work overtime on any weekend day if he chooses to. The problem is that he spends four hours on Saturday doing yard work around the house. He doesn't want to go to work *and* still have yard cleaning to do. It just seems like too much.

To make matters worse, he doesn't particularly like mowing the lawn or trimming the bushes or raking the leaves. He would like to be reading a good book or working on the bird houses which he makes and sells. Whether he goes to his job all day or does yard work for four hours, his Saturday still seems to be used up. Is there a better way?

Alex did the math. Eight hours times $21 is $168, or about $130 after taxes. This is what he would make if he worked a Saturday shift. With this in mind, he found a neighborhood boy who would do that four hours of yard work for $25.

He started to work one weekend day each month, taking home an extra $130. Since he was paying just $100 per month for the yard work (4 times $25), he was actually $30 further ahead. But more importantly, he had at least three out of four Saturdays completely free to do what he wanted.

This was time he spent reading, working on his birdhouses as a business, and relaxing. Soon he was making more money selling the things he made. He also spent one Saturday morning rearranging his finances, to spend less on everything, and make more money on his bank accounts.

Before long he didn't really need the overtime income, so he put it in an investment account. Once that reached $10,000, he stopped working weekends altogether, instead using one Saturday each month to better manage his investments - and to read good books.

He had his Saturdays free. He was doing more of the things he enjoyed. He was making more money. He had money to invest. And all this came from smart delegation.

Harry and Sue

Harry and his wife Sue were making minimum wage, and working too much. When the weekends came, they were busy with the kids. But Sue knew that there must be a better way. Despite their tight finances, she saved up $100, and paid her sister, who needed the money, to watch the kids for a Saturday and Sunday.

She told Harry they were going to spend the weekend looking at all of their financial options. First, she looked in the help wanted ads, eventually finding a job that paid just as much for a four-day schedule as what she was making working five days. She went to apply for it.

Later Harry mentioned some apartments nearby which cost $75 less per month than the one they were in, and were just as nice. By Sunday afternoon they had signed a lease that would save them $900 the first year alone. After reviewing their other expenses, they went online and found that they could get cheaper car insurance.

By the end of the weekend, they had found ways to cut their expenses by about $200 per month. They decided that they would start an investment account and put in $100 each month, and they would pay Sue's sister one weekend every month to watch the kids, so they could both relax and make better financial decisions.

Sue got the job that was just four days each week. She decided that the extra day freed up would be devoted to starting some kind of small business they could run from home. Two years later she was able to quit her job to concentrate on their business, and her friends were commenting on their good luck. All of this was made possible, of course, by Sue's decision to delegate the child care for a weekend and free up some time to do some smart thinking.

You understand the principle, but get creative in applying it. Think of any high-value actions you should take, but haven't had the time for. Then delegate low-value actions to free up the time necessary - even if this means paying someone.

It's easy to understand the value of delegation in business. A manager's time is too valuable to be spent mopping floors, right? He should be finding better ways to run the company. If he spends his time planning and making one or two smart decisions he can save or make the business tens of thousands of dollars, so why should he ever do low-wage work?

Apply the same principle to your personal life. Look for those activities that have the most value, and find the time for them by delegating less important responsibilities to someone else. More free time relaxes you, and makes you more open to the opportunities that present themselves. In other words, it leads to more good luck.

Some Notes On Delegating

Find the right people for the job. This means that you don't want to pay your friend's son to build your shed if he has little experience and you'll be fixing his mistakes. Find someone who can do the job right.

Look at the real values involved. $65 per hour for a plumber to fix your toilet may seem expensive, especially if you only make $14 per hour. But on the other hand, what if he get's the job done fast for $80, and it would take you two days because of inexperience? Unless you want to learn plumbing, you're better off paying the $80 and working an extra shift at your job.

Consider your realistic future earnings. When your business is still young and income low, you may want to do everything yourself instead of delegating work to a receptionist at $12-per-hour, thinking this will save you some money. But if the business will realistically be making you $40-an-hour for your effort before long, paying that $12 now can get you to that higher level sooner.

Remember these two basic principles:

1. Delegate things you're not proficient at to the experts.
2. Delegate lower-value tasks to make time for higher-value ones.

~ Secrets of Lucky People ~

Luck Exercise

List a few high-value things you haven't had time to do. These could include a trip to explore some ancient ruins if you're an amateur archeologist, or a new business you want to start, or something as simple as rearranging your savings and retirement accounts to make or save a few hundred dollars per year. Then list something that you can delegate to someone else in order to free up the time to do these more important things.

If money is an issue in your life at the moment, always start with the items that have the highest and quickest monetary return. For example, suppose a good budget and a plan to pay off your credit cards will save you $1000 per year, and you need a day to put it together. It's well worth letting someone take a shift for you at work, or paying $80 to have the house cleaned and the lawn mowed while you are busy with your plan. Start with these kinds of things.

I need time for: _____

I can delegate: _____

I need time for: _____

I can delegate: _____

I need time for: _____

I can delegate: _____

~ Steve Gillman ~

I need time for: _____

I can delegate: _____

Nothing is impossible if you can delegate.

- Anonymous

Chapter 24
Thomas Edison's Secret

Do What You Love

I never did a day's work in my life. It was all fun.

- Thomas Edison

Thomas Edison said the above despite working 18-hour days. If you actually get to follow your passions and make money doing it, you are almost lucky by definition, right? Doing what you want sure beats working for decades at jobs you hate. The really good news is that it can also be a decent recipe for financial success.

In 1960, psychologist Scrully Blotnik set up a study to track the lives of people who wanted to become wealthy. He started with 1,500 people, split into two groups.

The first group was the largest, with 1,245 people. These individuals each said that they would try to get rich first, and afterwards would pursue their passions. In other words, they planned to chase after money, hoping that this would someday make it easier to do the things they really wanted to do.

The second group had just 255 people. These individuals all said that they would follow their passions and interests first, and trust that money would come somehow. They shared a "Do what you love and the money will follow" philosophy.

What happened? Twenty years later Blotnik had lost track of a few hundred of the people, as can be expected. Some of them undoubtedly died or had moved and couldn't be located. But among the remaining people in the two groups, there were 83 millionaires.

Remember that all of the people in both groups said they wanted to be wealthy. These 83 millionaires were evidence that the desire to become wealthy can certainly help. In fact, about 8% of the people he could locate were millionaires, while at the time less than 1% of the general adult population were.

However, the really interesting part of the study is which group those millionaires came from. Of the 83, only one came from the first group, the people who said that they would try to get rich first, and afterwards would pursue their passions. 82 of them came from the smaller second group, the people who said they would follow their passions and interests first, and trust that money would come somehow.

That's a pretty amazing statistic, isn't it? 1 out of 1,245 became a millionaire in the first group, versus 82 out of 255 in the second. I'll do the math for you: This seems to indicate that you are 400 times more likely to become wealthy if you follow your passions rather than chase after money.

How To Follow Your Passions

The luckiest person is one whose passion and profession are the same.

- Anonymous

~ Secrets of Lucky People ~

It seems sometimes that you really can't follow your desires. At times this may even be true, in a limited sense. Perhaps you need a steady job right now, and don't have the time to pursue what you really want to do in life. On the other hand, often we are simply hesitating to change things for the better out of fear and uncertainty.

There are always ways to start pursuing your true interests and passions, even if you are temporarily in difficult circumstances. This doesn't mean you have to quit your job and risk everything on a new business you would enjoy - although that seems reasonable if you have no assets and a lousy job. It is all a matter of context. Sometimes small steps are called for, and sometimes large ones.

The following are some of the ways in which you can start following your passions without taking on unreasonable amounts of risk.

Rearrange Time

If we count, some of us will find that we spend a lot of hours in front of the television. If you really want to become a singer, a writer, or anything else, you can cut that time in half in order to find time for your passion. Setting aside one day per week can move you a long ways towards your goals in a few years time.

If you consolidate shopping into one or two trips per week, you might save hundreds of hours per year.

Getting higher quality sleep in order to spend an hour less in bed each night would free up 365 hours per year.

Make a list of your regular activities, and see if there is a way to eliminate any of them or reduce the time they take. Suppose you found ways to free up 2 hours and 45 minutes each day. That adds up to 1000 hours per year. What could you do with 1000 hours each year? Certainly something you enjoy, and maybe that will even lead to making money at some point.

Rearrange Finances

Many of us have $60 cable television bills. Is cable TV a higher priority than your true interests? $60 per month is $720 per year, which, by the way, is less than it took for my wife and I to start our internet business. The business now makes far more money than any job ever did for us, and it is based around our passion for writing and sharing information.

Directly financing the pursuit of your passions with money you save isn't the only option. You can also cut your expenses to buy time. Find a way to cut your monthly expenses by $200, and you can afford to work less. You might convince your boss to let you take unpaid time off each month, so you can do what you really want to do.

Still another option is to bank the savings from cost cutting for a few years and use it to make the break from your job. Cut costs by $260 per month and with interest you'll have about $20,000 in less than five years. That's enough to move where your dream job is, to start a small business or, if you budget well, to take a few months off to go surfing, if that's your thing.

I remember how nice it was many years ago when I paid off the mortgage on my first house and cut down from four days-per-week at my job (the most I had ever worked) to two or three. I had time to read, write, and plan trips. I also used the free time to explore ways to make my interests into businesses.

~ Secrets of Lucky People ~

Use Your Job

There are two ways to use your job to pursue your passions. The first is to find a way to be passionate about your work. Maybe there is some other position in the company that is more in line with your interests. Or perhaps you can search for a truly interesting job somewhere else while you keep this one for safety.

The other way is to simply see your job as a tool. All of your passions require time and sometimes money. Your job provides the money, which also buys time. See it as way to get what you want.

If you want to be a pilot, you can work extra shifts to pay for the lessons. If you want to dig for dinosaur bones, use your vacation time for that. If you need money for anything, you can ask for a raise, and then devote that new income to the pursuit of your passions.

Just Do It

When work is a pleasure, life is a joy. When work is duty, life is slavery.

- Maxim Gorky

I was a real estate agent from 1990 to 1991. I remember walking through nice homes with clients who loved this or that feature, and I could only nod in agreement while thinking, "It's just a house." Who cared if the floor was linoleum or Italian tile? Well, they did, but not I. To be honest, I had no interest in homes at all.

I thought that selling real estate would be a good way to make money. But what happens when you are in a business in which you have no interest other than the money? It's hard to do well, isn't it?

To be honest, I did start out well, and I made sales, but I absolutely hated most aspects of it. How lucky would it have been to succeed, but only by spending all my hours doing something I hated? And in any case, how likely would success be, if I had to continually motivate myself to do things that to me were boring, tedious and stressful? I quit after less than a year.

You can see that part of the reason people are more likely to succeed when they pursue their passion, is that motivation comes easily. How difficult is it to motivate yourself to climb a mountain as a paid guide if that is what you love to do? You wake up excited and ready to go. And whatever little chores you don't like are easier to do because they obviously get you what you really want.

Financial Success

Of course just doing what you want is no recipe for financial success. I love to write. I used to write stories and poetry and essays. But then I did nothing with them. Maybe three people read what I wrote in all those years. How does that help financially?

I even liked the idea of writing a novel. The average published writer of novels, however, makes something like $3,000 per year. You didn't read that wrong. There are relatively few writers that can make a living with novels.

I also love to play chess. I used to play for hours every Friday night at a local coffee shop. But even fewer chess players than writers can make a living at it.

You can't just pursue your passions in any way and think that money will follow. It just isn't realistic. But you can pursue your passions in ways that are more likely to lead to financial rewards. In my case, it turned out that

~ Secrets of Lucky People ~

writing online articles to promote web sites and selling e-books were the ways to make my writing pay.

If I wanted to pursue my interest in chess further and make money with it, I wouldn't even try to make a living from prize money. I'm not that good, and not willing to do what is necessary to become that good. On the other hand, I could write an e-book on chess and sell it, or I could start a business arranging chess tournaments or selling supplies.

The bottom line is that lucky people identify their passions and look for opportunities to pursue them. If they can't make money pursuing their interests in a certain way, they try another way, or they make money at something else to feed their passions. The one thing they don't do is make excuses.

Luck Exercise

List some interests and passions you have. Then after each, list a few ways you can make time for it, make money for it, and make money from it.

My passion or interest: _____

How I'll make time for it: _____

How I'll pay for it: _____

How it might make money: _____

My passion or interest: _____

How I'll make time for it: _____

~ Steve Gillman ~

How I'll pay for it: _____

How it might make money: _____

My passion or interest: _____

How I'll make time for it: _____

How I'll pay for it: _____

How it might make money: _____

> *Success is not the key to happiness. Happiness is the key to success. If you love what you are doing, you will be successful.*
>
> *- Herman Cain*

Chapter 25
Donald Trump's Secret

Continuing Education

He who is afraid of asking is ashamed of learning.

- Danish Proverb

Donald Trump and many other lucky people believe that much of their success is due to the habit of continuing to learn new things, especially from others. Trump, interestingly, likes to educate himself on more than just business. He reads self help and psychology books, as well as biographies, and about great philosophers. One of his continuing goals is to learn something new every day.

It will almost certainly help you to learn more about anything related to your career, business and investing goals. But don't stop there. Don't read only about your existing interests and hobbies.

You should also spend some time with books and people who can teach you something entirely new, outside of your usual interests.

~ Steve Gillman ~

My Favorite High School Dropouts

Education can mean traditional schooling and degrees. Many of the names of famous, wealthy and lucky individuals you see in this book have graduated from well-known universities. But formal education, while probably a big help, is not necessary for success. Just look at the following list of high school dropouts:

- Richard Branson - Billionaire British businessman. Founder of *Virgin Records* and dozens of other successful companies. I love the stories of his creative and bold approaches to business.
- Thomas Sowell - Economist, author and political commentator. One of my favorite writers on political and economic philosophy.
- Albert Einstein - Mathematician. He had much more than just a high IQ. He also had a great sense of humor and playful creative mind.
- George Carlin - Comedian. One of my favorite comedians, especially because of his fun with language and clichés.
- Billy Joel - Singer. A great entertainer.

Other famous high school dropouts include Jim Carrey, Tom Cruise, George Eastman, Randy Travis, John Travolta, Michael J. Fox, George Gershwin, Dhirubhai Ambani, Peter Jennings, Quentin Tarantino, Dave Thomas, Uma Thurman, and Ansel Adams.

On a recent Forbes Magazine list of billionaires, there were at least 18 who dropped out of high school. There are also 10 Nobel prize winners who are dropouts, as well as dozens of best-selling authors, several U.S. presidents, and some members of *Mensa*, the high-IQ group.

~ Secrets of Lucky People ~

That just covers some who quit high school. A list of famous and successful college dropouts couldn't fit on one page. It would include Bill Gates, the wealthiest man in the world as I write this.

This is not meant to suggest that formal education is without value. Certainly it is a necessity these days for certain professions. But the list above does suggest that a lack of formal credentials is no excuse for a lack of success. There are many ways to learn what you need to learn, and attending a university is just one of them.

Ways To Continue Your Education

Here are some examples of how you can have a lifetime of learning. You may want to start with subjects that relate to your goals, but mix in some general education on various things as well. You never know what may become useful.

Free Seminars

Of course these are designed to sell you a more expensive service or product, but you normally don't have to buy a thing, and if you do, it may be the best purchase of your life. In any case, I have found that there is always a lot to learn at these events. As I write this, my wife and I are planning to go to a Robert Kiyosaki *Rich Dad - Poor Dad* financial seminar.

Workshops

There are workshops on everything from building a better marriage to starting a business. These typically take place over a week or a weekend, although some are just a few hours long. They can be a great way to learn a lot in a little time, and are often very affordable.

Bookstores

I have learned everything from how to pick stocks to wilderness survival tips while sitting in bookstores and drinking coffee. I can't say for sure, but I would guess that the education from my hours spent in bookstores has been worth at least tens of thousands of dollars to me. Most large bookstores let you browse and read unbothered for hours, content with the occasional book purchase and the coffee and cookie sales.

The Public Library

There is a wealth of information and knowledge available at even small libraries. Many are online now, so you can reserve books from home and pick them up without having to search the stacks. The library has always been one of my favorite places to learn valuable things.

The Internet

You can get information on almost anything on the internet now. Learn how to use the search engines efficiently and you can quickly educate yourself on a subject. I tripled the response rate to one of my online newsletters after an hour of online research about marketing techniques.

E-books

You can buy e-books on everything from fishing techniques to how to have good luck, and they are available immediately. You can fit a whole library of books into your computer in this way. I credit one $17 e-book on search engine optimization with at least thousands of dollars in revenue for our business.

Magazines

Magazines are a great way to keep up on the latest trends and information in a given area, and they come right to your home. You can also read them for free at a library. I regularly use what I learn in magazines to better my life, and I've also created many income-producing web pages based on what I learned from them.

Newsletters

Not quite a magazine, but a more condensed form of information (usually without ads), these can be some of the best educational values out there. One six-page alternative health newsletter I paid $49 for (annually) told me about a truly effective six-dollar cure for a medical problem that the doctor had no solution for.

Email Newsletters and Courses

Most email newsletters and courses are free, and so have advertising to support them. But free or not, they are sometimes full of great ideas and advice. I personally produce email newsletters and courses on increasing your brainpower, investing in real estate, unusual ways to make money and a few others. I also subscribe to at least a dozen of these each year.

~ Steve Gillman ~

Home Study Courses

You've probably seen the testimonials of those who made a million dollars after buying some get-rich-quick course advertised on late night television, or turned their children into straight-A students after using some home-study program. There is hype and even outright lies out there, but some of these stories are real. I've taken a simple concept from a real estate book and used it to make thousands of dollars more than I would have without it, so I know the power of knowledge.

If it is a subject that interests you, take the chance for a couple hundred dollars. If you are uncertain, buy the ones with a money-back satisfaction guarantee. Then if it isn't worth it, you can send it back.

Television

You may have to wade through a lot of garbage to find good educational programming, but it's there. Various shows will teach you everything from treasure-hunting secrets to how to invent a new product or how to talk to your children.

Clubs and Organizations

If you want to learn about real estate investing, join a local investors club. To learn about stock market investing join a group like the American Association of Individual Investors. There are organizations for all sorts of interests, ranging from growing bonsai trees to exploring caves to writing books.

These can be one of the most cost effective ways to gain knowledge that is most useful, because these are people who are typically doing things and not just talking about doing them.

Continuing Education Classes

Many community colleges have non-credit classes on a variety of topics. These are designed for those with an interest in a subject, and almost always cost less than regular college classes. They range from classes on how to be an entrepreneur to how to use self-hypnosis, and usually take place once or twice a week in the evenings.

You'll notice that many of the suggestions listed above are free or almost free. This is on purpose. I want to take away in advance any excuses for not continuing one's education.

Learn By Listening To Others

A good listener is not only popular everywhere, but after a while he knows something.

- Wilson Mizner

Have you ever listened to an ideological argument? If you are normally a participant, take a break next time, and just listen. Whether it is about a political, social or ethical issue, if you listen honestly, and don't intrude, you'll probably be able to learn several new ideas from each side. You'll also probably be introduced to a few true and interesting facts by both.

There is usually an element of truth on each side of any serious argument. Each person is seeing things that the other doesn't see. They've had experiences that the other hasn't had. There really are reasons for their positions, even if not well thought out.

The participants in the argument usually don't learn much, however. Ego often prevents people from changing their minds when defending a position. The audience will almost always learn the most, so be in the audience more often. You'll be surprised at what you can learn.

Listening To Others - Part Two

Really listen and pay attention when people talk to you. It takes no more time than pretending to listen, and you might learn something useful. This was a difficult lesson for me. In the past I was more inclined to try to escape a conversation, in order to "do something."

Then, a few years back, my wife and I started a small business working the flea market circuit. We noticed right away that other vendors were always talkative. Most of it was small talk, ranging from the weather to where they lived. But often something useful was said, if we listened.

At first, my habitual response was to be polite, but try to get away. I wanted to use the time "productively." But to be honest, once our stand was set up, there wasn't all that much to do until the customers started coming around. So I started to visit with the other vendors, and to listen to them.

From one gentleman, we learned of an excellent market most vendors didn't know about. Once there, we made twice as much money as at any other flea market we had tried. Another vendor clued us in to selling used stuffed animals purchased from thrift stores. They became one of our best sellers. Listening to others, it turns out, was using time productively.

Of course, it can take practice to listen. Some of us are inclined to rush off and do something else. Slow down! Listening - especially to the right people, can be a very

~ Secrets of Lucky People ~

profitable (and enjoyable) activity. As you do it more often you get a good feel for who is worth listening too - and then you can get away from the time wasters.

Some of us also tend to dominate a conversation. This can be very nice for others if we are fonts of useful information. But the person speaking is not in a position to learn many new things, is he? To get over this habit, notice what percentage of the time you're speaking. Then start purposely going silent.

When you do speak up in a conversation, don't volunteer your opinion. Most people don't care. After all, if they want your opinion they'll ask for it. Instead, ask a question about something the other person has said. This is a better way to listen and to learn something new.

Learning From Lucky People

I used to live for much of the year in the Upper Peninsula of Michigan when I was younger. One result of this was that when I returned to Lower Michigan to visit friends and family, they would comment on my "accent." For example, I often used the expressions "eh" and "ya".

This happens when you spend more than a few months with those who speak a different dialect. In the same way, if you spend enough time with lucky people, their words and thoughts start to become your own. The more this happens, the luckier you are likely to become.

Bottom line: if you have some friends or acquaintances who are really lucky, happy people, spend more time with them.

Remember Max, the real estate investor from the lesson on priorities? I was fortunate to have worked with him long enough for some of his thinking processes to rub off on me. One thing in particular I remember was that he always looked at how to make things as easy as possible for someone to do what he (Max) wanted. This was true whether it was a seller or a buyer.

Years later, when I started renting rooms in my home, this idea was still with me. I made it easy for renters by including all utilities in the rent - no arguments about who owed what. I rented the rooms by the week or biweekly, according to when the renters received their paychecks - no budgeting required of them. I did everything to make it easy for them.

The result? I had happy renters that sometimes stayed for years, and always paid the rent. Making things easy for others in order to make a profit is an important principle. It became part of my business thought process due to my association with Max.

Learning From Imaginary Friends

What if there are no lucky people around to learn from? In that case, here's a nifty little technique that really works if you try it. Think of the luckiest person you have ever known well. This can even be a fictional character, as long as you can imagine him or her clearly in your mind. Then, whenever you are faced with a tough decision or a need for inspiration, just imagine what this person would do if he or she was in your situation. Mentally put the person in your body, if that helps.

You'll be amazed at how this activates the power of your unconscious mind. You might have no idea what to do about a decision or situation after a day of thought, and yet be able to see in ten seconds what this "lucky" person would do. You'll get solutions and thoughts you would never normally have without the assistance of this imagined helper.

~ Secrets of Lucky People ~

Learning The Right Lessons

What we actually learn, from any given set of circumstances, determines whether we become increasingly powerless or more powerful.

- Blaine Lee

It is just common sense that you will have a better life if you learn from your experiences and those of others. But do you know what is worse than learning nothing from an experience? Learning the wrong lessons.

Suppose you have to give a speech. You're poorly prepared and just hope you'll come up with something interesting to say to the audience. The speech goes horribly. You're nervous, the audience is bored, and as soon as you are done you just want to forget the whole thing.

Of course whether you try to forget it or not, it affects you. The truth is that we can't help but learn something from - and be affected by - every experience we have. In this case, you might have learned one or all of the following:

- You hate public speaking.
- Public speaking is a waste of time.
- You are a bad speaker.
- People don't understand you.

Disempowering lessons like these are sometimes less than conscious, but they can stay with you and affect the quality of your life.

They stay with you, that is, unless you chose to consciously learn empowering lessons. In this case, those might include the following lessons:

- You could like speaking, once you're better at it.
- You can be better prepared before giving a speech.
- There are better ways to get your points across.

The more empowering lessons are those truths which widen your options. Don't let your unconscious mind and emotions be your only teachers in the classroom of personal experience. Consciously choose to identify the lessons that are most useful. Be your own teacher.

Three Luck Exercises

1. Continuing Education: Listening

Practice listening to a conversation without saying too much. Ideally, listen while two or three others talk. Try to say nothing unless you ask a question, or are asked one yourself. Then write down something new and interesting that you learned, followed by some way in which you might use the information.

This may seem silly, but writing it down tells your unconscious mind that listening for these new and useful ideas is important, and so "programs" it to do so more automatically.

What I Learned When I Listened: _____

_____

_____

What I Learned When I Listened: _____

~ Secrets of Lucky People ~

_____

_____

2. Continuing Education: Lucky People

List the three luckiest people you know. Think of a few things that are going on in your life, and imagine how these individuals might approach them differently. Then make a point to spend some time or talk on the phone with at least one of them.

The Three Luckiest People I Know

_____

_____

_____

3. Continuing Education: The Right Lessons

Identify a "wrong" lesson or two you have learned from some circumstances or events in the past, and replace them with better lessons which can be drawn from the same happenings.

Wrong Lesson: _____

_____

~ Steve Gillman ~

Better Lesson: _____

_____

Wrong Lesson: _____

_____

Better Lesson: _____

_____

There is no such thing as a worthless conversation, provided you know what to listen for. And questions are the breath of life for a conversation.

- James Nathan Miller

Chapter 26
Richard Branson's Secret

Taking Risks

Often the difference between a successful person and a failure is not one has better abilities or ideas, but the courage that one has to bet on one's ideas, to take a calculated risk - and to act.

- Andre Malraux

When billionaire Richard Branson started *Virgin Records*, he was barely an adult. One of his first big hits was Mike Oldfield's *Tubular Bells*. It was a runaway best seller, especially after the music was used in the soundtrack of the movie *The Exorcist*.

In his book, *Screw It, Let's Do It*, Branson says that people would comment on how lucky he was to have a hit like this, especially at such a young age in a new business. Why was he able to sign such a great composer before the other bigger labels got him?

The truth is that the other labels were afraid to take the risk. *Tubular Bells* was synthesized music of a type that had never before been popular. In fact, every other record label had turned the opportunity down already.

Perhaps *Virgin Records* had less to lose, since they needed to sign some group soon or close the business. There's a lesson about risk right there: You have less to lose when starting out, so take your risks early.

In any case, Branson was willing to do it. This wasn't a case of a great opportunity falling into his lap instead of another's.

This was an opportunity that went knocking on every door - Branson was the only one who chose to answer - and to risk investing in it.

A Two-Part Lesson

You can't win the lottery if you don't play, right? The first half of this lesson then, is that to get lucky, you have to be playing the game. You have to take a risk. Of course you probably won't win the lottery even if you do play, because the odds are so terrible.

The second half of the lesson, then, is to play the right games. The lottery isn't one you should normally play.

Having worked in a casino for years when I was younger, I can tell you that most people have no idea how to judge risk versus reward when gambling. Still, to this day, I know many gamblers who regularly win thousands of dollars. This will happen to you too if you play in casinos often, and bet enough money.

Unfortunately, those same people lose hundreds of dollars many other times. The net result? Most lose more money than they win in the long run. This is because they only understand the first part of risk taking - that to win, you have to play the game.

The good players are different. They often lose too, but they win more than they lose, because they understand the

~ Secrets of Lucky People ~

second part of risk-taking. They know how to play the right games.

For example, if you play slot machines, hoping to get rich, you're playing the wrong game. The right ones have odds in your favor. In a casino this might include blackjack - but only if you know how to "count cards." You might also play roulette, if you know how to "chart the wheel." Poker can be a good bet too, if you can play well enough to beat the other players and overcome the casino's cut.

In other areas of life, it's tough to precisely determine the "odds" of success. But if you want better luck, you should understand the process.

Learn To Evaluate Risks And Rewards

Smart poker players do some mathematical analysis before they put their bet in the pot. They analyze "investment odds," which are based on the probability that the hand will win, the amount of the bet, and the amount of the potential win. For example, suppose you have four hearts in a game of draw poker. To keep this simple, we'll say that the odds of drawing a fifth heart *and* winning the hand are 1-in-5, and you need to call a bet of $20 to stay in the game.

Should you bet?

We can't say. All we know at this point is that you have a 20% chance to win the hand if you make the bet. But what do you win in relation to your bet? This is important, because this isn't about just the risk, but about the risk/reward ratio.

If the pot will total over $100, it's a good bet, because the investment odds are in your favor. This means that in the long run, you'll win more than you lose by betting $20 to win more than $100 when the odds of winning are 1-in-

5, or 20%. If the pot will be less than $100, you should fold.

To understand this better, suppose you can win $120 on the hand. If you play fifty such hands, you would expect to win ten (1-in-5). That's $1,200, or $1,000 after deducting the $200 you bet. The forty hands you lose will cost you $800 ($20 x 40), so you can see that you would expect to win more than you lose.

You don't have to do this kind of analysis for most of life's decisions, nor can you. You'll never have enough information to put definite numbers on most things. Even in poker there is much that can't be quantified. Does that smile on Jack's face mean a 75% or 55% probability that he drew to his inside straight? The exact odds and the math to get there are not the important lesson (but they help if you want to win at poker).

It is the principle that matters here. You can't just ask, "Am I more likely to succeed or fail if I try this?" You have to look at three things: the risk, the reward, and the odds of success.

I knew a man who lost 26 out of every 27 spins on the roulette wheel, but he won $80,000 before he was done (many months later). How is this possible? He lost $10 on the losing spins and won $350 on every winning spin.

On the other hand, let's suppose that according to race track statistics the favorite horse "shows" (comes in first, second or third place) 9 out of ten times. Should you bet on the favorite to show? You'll win nine-out-of-ten times, but whether or not this is a good bet depends on what you will win.

I rarely gamble, but I once bet four dollars on the favorite horse to "show" when I was dragged to a race by friends. My horse came in second, so I won. But when I went to collect, I was handed just $4.25 for my ticket - a profit of 25 cents! At that rate, if I won my bet nine of every ten times, I would lose consistently. For every ten races I would lose $4 once and win 25-cents nine times ($2.25), for a net loss of $1.75.

You see, you can lose most of the time and be a winner. You can also win most of the time and be a loser. You have to look at the whole picture. You have to look at the risk/reward ratio. Now let's look at a more common example; deciding what kind of business to start.

Getting Lucky In Business

Suppose you want to start a business, and you have narrowed you choices to a restaurant, an internet business, or a cleaning business. They all have the potential, and roughly the same probability, to eventually make your income goal of $80,000 per year. Unfortunately, they also all normally fail for half of the people who start them.

Does this mean they are equally good bets? You can't say until you look at the whole picture. Perhaps the cleaning business or internet business will only require a risk of a few hundred dollars, and starting the restaurant will risk your $50,000 life savings.

Hmm... Risk $50,000 or risk $500 to accomplish the same thing, with about the same odds of success? This analysis makes the decision look easy, right? Even if the restaurant was much more likely to succeed than the internet or cleaning business, the risk/reward ratio would probably be much better for the latter two. On the way to success, you could even afford to fail several times at businesses that only require an investment of a few hundred dollars.

Of course, this simplifies life too much. You could also fail forever because you're starting businesses you hate, ones that leave you unmotivated. The odds of success are also determined by your own desires, efforts and character. Maybe you have the experience and desire to make a restaurant work.

And the value of rewards are personal. Some things are worth more to you than to others. Writing articles and making web sites is certainly worth more to me in non-monetary ways than running a restaurant, so I would do it even if it meant a lower income. Running a restaurant sounds awful to me.

In other words, risk-taking in life is not as exact a science as it is in poker. It's a very intuitive process. However, this doesn't mean you can't think about it rationally, as well. The relevant point here is that you need to have your mind thinking the right way, looking at risk, reward and probabilities. With that thought process as a habit, even your intuitive hunches become better.

Don't Put All Your Eggs In One Basket

The successful always has a number of projects planned, to which he looks forward. Any one of them could change the course of his life overnight.

- Mark Caine

Lucky people usually have several things going at once, which increases the odds of some sort of success. For example, if a writer is writing a novel, and writing articles for magazines, and spending a few hours each week building a web site, he has three things that might start to make him some money and help him towards his goals.

Just as you normally shouldn't put all of your money into one investment, you shouldn't invest all your time and effort into one goal. Have alternatives, and keep them alive with some occasional thought and work. One of them might be your lucky break.

Take Small Risks

Don't be afraid to go out on a limb. That's where the fruit is.

- H. Jackson Brown

With big risks, there are no easy answers to which are appropriate. Small risks, on the other hand, often have rewards that clearly outweigh the amount of the risk. Take a lot of these small risks, and you'll not only get lucky more often, but you'll also get practice for the big decisions.

For example, a single woman might risk feeling or looking foolish, if she asks a stranger for a date. But how much does she really lose compared to what she might gain? She will feel bad for a few minutes at most, but she could find the love of her life, right? This is an example of a small risk with a large potential reward.

Suppose you're interested in acting, but not sure that you have what it takes. A small risk would be to take the time to try out for a role in a local play. It is possible that you won't do well, and that you'll feel embarrassed - that's the entire risk. On the other hand, this could lead to a very rewarding new career.

Should you spend $100 on that real estate course or internet seminar? If you're interested in a given business, the answer is almost certainly yes. It is a small risk to take for a large potential profit, isn't it?

I paid $80 for an e-book that showed how to make more money by reformatting the advertising on my web sites. I also risked the several hours it took to implement the advice. I figured if the ideas in that little 64-page book could boost my revenue by $20 per month, it would be well worth it. The actual improvement was at least $300 more per month with no additional work after that initial effort. Small risks can pay big.

True Story

My wife Ana and I were considering starting an internet business a few years back. We hesitated while we wrapped up another business that hadn't done so well. Then I saw a commercial for a video that taught a system for building a website and selling an e-book. I bought it for about $50. It convinced us to finally build a web site.

Interestingly, we never did start selling e-books until much later. Nonetheless, it was that video which got us motivated to start. I might otherwise still be at the post office or the casino where I used to work. Instead, I get to write about whatever I want and make more money than ever before. Now there's a good example of a small risk that paid off.

Of course I had bought a few money-making schemes before. I had invested a couple thousand dollars over the years in information products. Did they all work? No, but that's okay, isn't it? If you spend a few thousand dollars on your way to making a million, will it bother you in the end?

You see, when you understand risk and reward, it becomes clear that you can lose most of your bets and still be a winner. One good book could pay for all the money wasted on less useful ones.

My personal observation: Books and other education and information products, whether on making money, building a better relationship, or almost any other subject,

~ Secrets of Lucky People ~

have just about the best risk/reward ratio of any investments you can make.

Proper Risk Taking - A Review

1. Get In The Game

You won't get lucky in love if you stay home alone. You won't have good luck as an author if you don't submit your novel to publishers. You won't make money in the stock market if you don't buy stocks. Risk attracts luck, good and bad. Take a risk.

2. Play The Right Game

You won't consider love lucky, if you're with the wrong person. You won't get published if you approach the wrong publishers. You won't often make winning bets on stocks if you don't invest in an area you have studied. Understand risk versus reward.

3. Play More Than One Game

If you want to be lucky in love, try joining some interesting group while also going out with friends. If you want to be a writer, try doing articles, books and perhaps an online blog. If you want to make money in stocks, invest in several different industries. Don't put all your eggs in one basket.

Luck Exercise

List several risks you could take to get what you want in life. Look honestly at each and answer three questions:

- How much would I risk here? (Include your time, money, mental energy, and anything else that could be lost.)
- What are my odds of success? ("Not so good," "okay," "good," and "very good" can be used, rather than percentages.)
- What is the likely and/or possible reward? (Money, love, personal growth, sense of satisfaction, and anything else of value.)

Pick one and take a risk this week.

Note: Precise calculation is unrealistic in most of life's decisions. The point is simply to train your intuition in the right approach. For example, many good poker players don't consciously compute all the odds, but they are doing the same thing intuitively. They might simply feel, "I probably will lose this hand, but it seems like a worthy enough risk to win a big pot."

A Risk I Could Take: _____

Quantify and specify the risk: _____

Probability of success: _____

Potential reward: _____

A Risk I Could Take: _____

Quantify and specify the risk: _____

Probability of success: _____

~ Secrets of Lucky People ~

Potential reward: _____

A Risk I Could Take: _____

Quantify and specify the risk: _____

Probability of success: _____

Potential reward: _____

I've found that luck is quite predictable. If you want more luck, take more chances.

- Brian Tracy

Chapter 27
Ben's Bad Luck Turns Good

Self Talk

The inner speech, your thoughts, can cause you to be rich or poor, loved or unloved, happy or unhappy, attractive or unattractive, powerful or weak.

- Ralph Charell

"How could you do something so stupid? What were you thinking?" Ben listened to the insults and hung his head. He tried to get back to work, but he no longer felt motivated. He had chased away what could have been the biggest sale since he started as a real estate agent. He made the mistake of talking about the homes he liked, rather than listening to what the couple had to say.

"I guess you're going to be the worst in the office again this month." Ben sighed and arranged his desk. He thought about how much he enjoyed working in real estate at first. He wasn't liking it now. "Because you can't sell anything!" He would have stopped listening to the nasty comments, except they were coming from his own mind.

~ Secrets of Lucky People ~

One day he realized what he was doing to himself. His own thoughts had convinced him that he didn't know how to sell real estate, and as a result, he was always looking for evidence of that. Of course, he found it. We always find what we are looking for in matters like these. He wondered what would happen if he stopped paying attention to the critical remarks, and started saying something more useful.

The next time he started to talk too much with a buyer, he heard the voices in his head saying how stupid he was, and he countered them by consciously thinking, "No, I'm actually very smart, but I sometimes make unconscious mistakes. And now that I'm aware of this process, I can learn something valuable here."

He asked the buyer a question, and then another. He listened carefully, and soon had a clear idea of what the man was looking for. He found several homes for sale that met his criteria, and eventually sold him one. Buyers always appreciate an agent that listens well and shows them only homes that fit their needs.

The next time his listening skills failed him, he told himself, "I can make this experience into something profitable." He sat down and designed a questionnaire for buyers. He had it put into real estate guides, telling readers that if they filled it out and sent it to him, he would let them know about any properties that fit their criteria - and nothing else. Buyers liked this, and he soon had more business than ever.

Ben still heard the nasty comments in his own mind from time to time, but now he understood that they were useless. Every time he heard one, he quickly replaced it with a more useful thought. He soon was doing better as a real estate agent, and was happier as well.

~ Steve Gillman ~

What Is Self Talk?

It is something we all do. We are always explaining things to ourselves, and making comments to ourselves. The real question is, what are we saying, and does it matter?

It does. What you say to yourself radically affects the quality of your life, and your ability to do things effectively. Self-talk is thought, and the way you think affects the way you feel and the way you act, so it leads directly to what can be called bad luck or good luck.

Are you using primarily positive self-talk or negative self-talk? Some of the things that positive and negative people say follow. Look closely at the difference. When you do, you'll immediately see how these "mere words" can affect your life.

Negative Self Talk

Negative people explain bad things by internalizing them ("It's me again."). They consider them permanent ("It's always this way."). They generalize ("Life sucks."). When they explain good things, they externalize them ("That's just lucky."), consider them temporary ("That went well *today*."), and see them only in a specific context ("At least *this* went right.").

- "It's *always* a mess when I meet someone new."
- "This party is great, not like mine."
- "This is fun for now."
- "Well, *that* went okay, I guess."
- "I screwed up again."
- "This good weather won't last."

~ Secrets of Lucky People ~

Positive Self Talk

Positive people explain bad things by externalizing them ("It was just the weather."). They consider them temporary ("That was a rough couple hours."). They see them as isolated ("*That* part of the plan didn't work, but..."). When they explain good things, they internalize ("Life is great!"), consider them to be more or less permanent changes ("Now I know how to do this."), and generalize from them ("Things are working out well.").

- "I've done well with this."
- "I like the way things are going."
- "This has become a great business to be in."
- "That just went bad due to the weather."
- "It was rough for an hour or two."
- "The car broke down, but the trip was fun."

Why not explain things to yourself in a positive constructive way? You'll see a difference in your attitude today. When you make a positive internal dialog your normal mode of operation, you'll see a difference in your life. One of the quickest and simplest ways to change your experience of life is to change your self talk.

Self Talk - Part Two

Self-suggestion makes you master of yourself.

- W. Clement Stone

In addition to being important to your self esteem, what you are saying to yourself also more directly affects what you can do. It does this by forming your beliefs about what is possible for you and what isn't. But can thoughts make things possible? Of course they can.

One night we were watching ice skaters competing in the Nationals. As they showed some old films from 35 years ago, it occurred to me that today's skaters are doing amazing things that back then were definitely considered to be impossible. How is this so? We know that humans haven't physically evolved that much in one generation - but our beliefs have.

For hundreds of years nobody could run a mile in under four minutes. Then in 1954 Roger Bannister did it. Soon others could repeat his achievement, and now it has become common. Again, people's bodies didn't evolve, but their thoughts did. Beliefs matter.

Why would you try something if you really believed it wasn't possible to succeed? How could you keep looking for new ways to succeed if you thought it was impossible? Beliefs matter, and they are crucial to our motivation.

Affirmations?

The usual and most direct way to change your beliefs about yourself is through affirmations. You repeat the beliefs that you want to program into your unconscious in the present tense. You might stand in front of the mirror every morning, for example, and repeat 20 times, "I am a successful businessman," or "People like me," or the classic, "Every day in every way I am getting better and better."

There are studies that demonstrate the effectiveness of affirmations, but they don't seem to work for everyone. Perhaps every time you repeat, "I am lucky," or "I am beautiful," your unconscious mind is saying "No you're not," and canceling out the effect. If they work for you, use them, but there is another way.

~ Secrets of Lucky People ~

Evidence is a more powerful persuader than affirmations. If you want to develop a belief that you are lucky, for example, look for evidence of your luck. Any examples, however small, will make it more believable when you tell yourself "I'm a lucky person." This is especially true if you make the positive statement while looking right at the evidence.

As I explain in more detail in the chapter on attracting luck, this looking for evidence also makes it more noticeable. Look for red cars for a few days, and by day three you'll start to see them all over. That's the way the brain works, so using it in that way to change what you believe makes sense.

Luck Exercise

List a few negative things you find yourself saying in your mind. Challenge these with questions, like "Is this really true? How could this be wrong?" Take notes. Then replace each with a more positive thing you can tell yourself. This is a powerful way to break the habit of negative self talk.

Negative Self Talk: _____

Evidence That It Isn't True: _____

A More Positive Truth: _____

Negative Self Talk: _____

Evidence That It Isn't True: _____

~ Steve Gillman ~

A More Positive Truth: _____

Negative Self Talk: _____

Evidence That It Isn't True: _____

A More Positive Truth: _____

Negative Self Talk: _____

Evidence That It Isn't True: _____

A More Positive Truth: _____

Men often become what they believe themselves to be. If I believe I cannot do something, it makes me incapable of doing it. But when I believe I can, then I acquire the ability to do it even if I didn't have it in the beginning.

- Mahatma Gandhi

Chapter 28
Imagining A Business Into Existence

Visualization

Visualization is daydreaming with a purpose.

- Bo Bennett

Jackie and Tina both wanted to start a small business of some sort. Tina thought about it just like that, as "a small business of some sort." Jackie, on the other hand, spent time thinking about what kind she wanted.

She did more than that, though. Once she decided that she was interested in running a clothing store, she started to visualize it. She saw the racks of clothes. She imagined the dressing rooms, clean and carpeted, with good lighting and mirrors. She saw the people milling about, looking at the newest items, smiling, and coming to the counter to buy things.

Meanwhile, Tina looked around for possible business ideas. When she did narrow her choices down to a service business of some sort, she listed some possibilities: house cleaning, window washing, dog walking. She kept meaning to take the next step, but never did. It is tough to be motivated when you aren't even sure what you want.

Jackie made plans for her business. She visualized the process as well. She imagined seeing a "for rent" sign on a downtown storefront, and imagined herself talking to the owner about a lease. In her mind, she even listened to telephone conversations with suppliers.

One day, she saw a vacant store which would be perfect. She had missed it before, but the regular visualization had made her more sensitive to the various empty buildings. And because she had imagined it so many times, she found it relatively easy to call up the owner and ask about the place. A year later she was doing well with her new clothing store, while Tina was still undecided about what kind of business to start.

Successful people often see what they want in their minds. They hear the waves lapping at the beach if they want to be in Hawaii. They feel the pull of the "big one" on the line if a fishing trip is their goal. Visualization, and vivid imagination using all of your senses, helps you get what you want in four basic ways - and none of them are about the mystical nonsense sold in books on "manifesting." (At least the mystical part is nonsense.) There are rational reasons visualization can help, and you can verify these for yourself.

Why Visualization Works

1. **Motivation**

   What the mind can conceive and believe it can achieve.

   - Napoleon Hill

~ Secrets of Lucky People ~

Visualization helps motivate you towards your goals and gives you energy to do something about them. The more vivid the experience, the more profound the result. Vividly imagining something you would really like causes mental and physical changes. You can demonstrate this for yourself with a simple experiment.

Go look in a mirror at your eyes. There should be enough light to see your pupils clearly. Now vividly imagine something you desire. A person or a place works best. In your mind, see, hear, smell and touch the scene. You will notice that your pupils get larger almost immediately.

This little experiment just hints at all the chemical changes going on in your brain. Just as talking about something you are passionate about can give you energy, so can imagining the things you want. Visualization is motivating on both a mental and physical level.

2. New Ideas

Try out your ideas by visualizing them in action.

- David Seabury

Another thing that visualization can do for you is give you new ideas, and new ways to get what you want. This has long been used as a problem-solving technique. The effect is more pronounced the more clearly you can see things in your mind, so exercise that imagination.

In order to have an example, I just stopped to think about my goal to sell more e-books. I imagined a reader of my book sitting at her computer. For some reason she got up, and was obviously annoyed that she couldn't take the book with her. Immediately it occurred to me that if it came with a downloadable audio version, she could save it to a

CD and listen in her car.

This is not a new idea in the marketplace, but it is new for me. It might increase sales. Notice that once I started the process, the imagery took on a life of its own. I didn't tell her to get up from in front of that computer.

This is the power of the unconscious at work. There is a lot of processing going on in our minds that we are not aware of, and visualization is a way to access more of that power.

As a simple experiment, try imagining some situation you would like in the future, at least a couple years from now. Then imagine how you got there.

Short scenes might come to mind, like a quick review of a past episode of a television show. See if you can make sense of the steps that brought you to that desired place. Note what new ideas the process gives you.

3. Mental Practice

> *I've discovered that numerous peak performers use the skill of mental rehearsal of visualization. They mentally run through important events before they happen.*
>
> *- Charles A. Garfield*

Visualization can also directly improve your performance in life. This is due in part to the increase in confidence that comes from imagining your actions over and over. But vividly imagining successful actions also creates real changes in the body and mind.

In one famous experiment, psychologist Alan Richardson tested three groups of people to see how well they threw "free throws" with a basketball. All groups were tested on the first and twentieth days. The first group practiced every day during those 20 days. The second group did nothing. The third group did no actual practice, but spent 20 minutes each day visualizing successful free throws.

After 20 days, the first group had improved their successful throws by 24%. Not surprisingly, the second group didn't improve. The third group, however, those who had simply visualized their free throws, improved by 23% - almost as much as those that actually practiced.

Richardson noted that those who did best didn't just "see" the free throws in their minds. They also "felt" the ball and "heard" it bounce. When physiologist Edmund Jacobson did a study in which participants visualized athletic activities, he found subtle movements in the muscles which corresponded to what the muscles would do if the imagined activity was real.

In other words, visualization is similar to "real" practice. When you vividly imagine actions, you are making real changes in your mind and body. You are making neuronal and muscular connections, just like you do when you actually repeat the actions physically.

4. Tuning In

When you visualize what you want, you are telling your mind to be aware of certain things and to bring those things to your attention. As explained in the chapter on attracting luck, this is a way to get the reticular cortex working for you. In the story above, Jackie's eye catches the empty store downtown because her visualization exercises have caused her to "tune into" such potential opportunities.

~ Steve Gillman ~

Using Visualization

Try to imagine things in detail. If, for example, you are hoping to find a better job, see yourself filling out applications and smiling across the desk from your new boss.

At the same time, don't get too hung up on one image (unless you are practicing a specific skill). Seeing several possible outcomes opens your mind to more possibilities, and keeps you from getting disappointed because you didn't get exactly what you wanted.

If you have a hard time visualizing things (I do), practice. You can look at a room or a scene outdoors, then close your eyes and try to see it in detail in your mind. Do this until it gets easier.

The potential applications for your new visualization skills are everywhere. Want to be luckier in love? Imagine yourself smiling confidently at a man or woman you would like to meet. Want to be a better skier? Repeated visualization can improve your performance when the opportunity arises for real. Start visualizing!

Luck Exercise

List several things you would like to happen in your life. For each, vividly imagine the situation, and perhaps the process that lead to it. Notice which parts of the visualization are most motivating, and what new ideas you get. After each item on the list make a note or two about the experience.

A Situation I Would Like: _____

Notes: _____

~ Secrets of Lucky People ~

A Situation I Would Like: _____

Notes: _____

A Situation I Would Like: _____

Notes: _____

A Situation I Would Like: _____

Notes: _____

See yourself confronting your fears in your mind's eye and handling those fears like a champ.

- Les Brown

Chapter 29
Climbing Mount Everest

Goals

Without goals, and plans to reach them, you are like a ship that has set sail with no destination.

- Fitzhugh Dodson

Randy and Norman both had the same goal: to climb Mount Everest. They lived in Chicago. They were both in their twenties and in decent health. They also had some experience climbing, so they knew they could handle it if they had a chance. They were friends briefly before going their separate ways.

Norman told people about his goal. He figured that he could find a way to do it in the next four or five years, once he had made some money. As much as he wanted to summit Everest, though, he didn't bother to write down the goal or any of the necessary steps which would get him there.

Five years later he was thirty years old, and he was still living in Chicago. He had been making a good income for

~ Secrets of Lucky People ~

many years, but he hadn't saved any of it. He still dreamed of going to climb Everest, but for now he was starting a new corporate job where he would be paid more. It wasn't a job he would enjoy, but then it would mean eventually making enough money to pay for his dreams.

Twenty years after that, Norman had a good position in a large company. He made more money than most of his friends, and had a nice house to show for it, along with a nice car and other things. He was fifty years old, and still hadn't been anywhere near Mount Everest. In fact, he was still dreaming about traveling the world, buying a fishing lodge, and the other wishes he called goals.

Randy, on the other hand, wrote down his goal to climb Mount Everest the moment he decided on it. He specified how much money it would take, and figured out what annual and monthly savings goals he would have to meet in order to pay for it in six years. He set up a special investment account to put the money into. He created a list of lesser goals or steps, including getting in better shape, finding ways to cut the cost of the trip, and learning all about the mountain.

Over the next few years he worked through the goals one-by-one. He read every book he could on Everest, and he regularly spent time looking at photos of the mountain and at the routes that others had taken. He started to buy the necessary equipment and clothing one piece at a time. He used his vacation time to go to Mount Ranier in Washington State, to be guided to the top - as practice for his Everest climb.

As he accomplished each of these things, he checked them off his list, and made any necessary changes to his plans according to what he had learned.

He never did make much money, but he consistently put aside some for his goal. His investments worked out better than he had expected, and he had the funding for his Everest trip within five years. About the time Norman was starting his corporate job, five years after deciding he would like to climb Everest, but still without a plan or a penny set aside, Randy was standing on top of the world at the summit of the highest mountain on Earth.

Norman was fifty years old when he read an article about Randy in an outdoor magazine. He had read about the Everest climb twenty years earlier, and about his former friend's many other adventures, which now included an outdoor equipment company he had just started. He gave him a call to congratulate him - and to ask him how he did it all.

The next morning Norman went to the bank and opened an account to start saving for his fishing lodge. Afterwards, he put a check next to "open bank account" on his goal sheet.

Goals work if you work your goals.

Setting Goals Properly

I understand the quote at the start of this chapter (*Without goals, and plans to reach them, you are like a ship that has set sail with no destination. - Fitzhugh Dodson*), but to be honest I often like the idea of a trip without destination. It can be nice to wander and explore without a clear plan. Some of the best gifts life has given me are things I didn't know I wanted and places that were not my planned destinations.

On the other hand, when I do know what I want, and when I do have a destination in mind, I know what I need to do. I sit down and properly set goals. Why? Because it works.

I haven't found research to confirm that lucky people

are more likely to set goals, but it makes sense. Certainly goal setting has been shown repeatedly to result in more income and assets. Good goals get you more of what you want, and that might be considered good luck. But why does it sometimes seem like personal goal setting doesn't work?

One reason is that people often simply wish for things and situations. They call these goals, and then are disappointed when they don't get them. This isn't effective goal setting (actually, they are really just wishes and daydreams). Good goals have at least some of the following:

1. They're specific.

"I want to be healthy" is just too general. "I want to lose this gut, eat healthier food and walk three times a week," is better. Goals need to be more specific so we can see more clearly where we are going and know how close we are getting, which leads us to the next requirement:

2. They're measurable.

How many pounds will you lose? How much money will you make? How will you know when your relationship is better? Think the latter can't be measured? How about counting the times you fight, and the hours you enjoy being together. Make the goal to cut the weekly total in half for the first and double the second. There is almost always a way to measure progress, even if it is an imperfect measurement.

3. They're written down.

There's power in writing down goals. It makes them

more real. This is how you "program" your subconscious mind, especially if you review your goals regularly.

4. They're realistic.

Even if it is possible to become an astronaut, if you're 55, you better try becoming a pilot for now. Unrealistic goals just set you up for failure. That said, don't let others tell you what's unrealistic for you.

5. They have definite deadlines.

By what date will you have that new job? When will you start that book you're going to write, be half done, and be finished? Setting dates helps. It isn't so important that you meet those deadlines. The point of having them is to make the commitment real, and the progress measurable.

6. They're made into plans.

It might seem overwhelming to have a goal like circling North America in a canoe. But buying a map, and then a canoe isn't so difficult. Putting aside $50 this week is achievable. Paddling along the coast the first day isn't too tough either. Making goals into specific plans and steps makes their achievement more likely. It isn't so overwhelming to take one step at a time.

7. They're well-motivated.

Having a goal for the right reason is a good start. If you actually enjoy real estate investing, you'll be more likely to meet your goal to make a million doing it, because you'll have more inherent motivation. You should also learn how to re-motivate yourself when you lose the excitement (more on that coming up), and you should reward yourself when you make progress, especially when you reach significant milestones.

8. They take into account personal factors.

Sometimes your psychology or beliefs aren't right for a goal. For example, if your goal is to be a millionaire, and you feel like wealthy people are somehow bad, you need to change your beliefs or how you feel about money. Good goal setting considers personal changes that are necessary or useful, and incorporates them into the plan.

9. They're followed by action.

If you want to hike the Appalachian Trail next year, and you just added it to your list of goals, set down that pen and take a walk today. Buy a book on hiking tomorrow. Take a walk with a heavy backpack three times next week. An important key to motivation and to getting where you want to be is to start with any movement towards the goal. Action begets action. Start slowly if necessary, but start.

10. They're not written in stone.

Goals naturally evolve, as new information becomes available. Why continue to work towards your goal to become a doctor once you learn that you like doing lab work better? Make a new goal.

The last one can be a tough one. An excuse isn't the same thing as a change of course, but to know the difference in oneself requires a certain level of self-awareness. Make developing that awareness one of your "preparatory goals." Then apply these ten keys to personal goal setting, and you'll get to where you want to be.

How well does goal setting work? Just 3% of the graduating class of Yale University had clearly defined written goals when researchers polled them in 1953. Twenty years later all the 1953 graduates who could be located were polled again. It was found that the 3% who had clearly defined and written goals had more wealth than all the other 97% put together.

I am sure that many of those in the 3% were considered to be very "lucky" by others and by themselves. And once again, we see that luck is not just something people are born with. In this case it is at least partly the result of making written goals.

A Note About Goal Setting

Here's a little secret you don't hear from most "success coaches": Making specific goals too soon can backfire. This is because you may not have done the self-work necessary to be ready for a goal, and you may not really know yet which goals are good for you.

Years ago, when I used to write down specific financial targets, for example, I hit them, but I made myself miserable in the process. I'm often happier and more relaxed if I take a clear direction, and then let the goals formulate themselves in time. Then I write them down. Setting specific goals in writing is a powerful way to make progress, but it's up to you to decide when it is appropriate.

~ Secrets of Lucky People ~

Luck Exercise

List several values you have. These can be very general, like "freedom," "travel," "love," or "financial security." Then make some short-term and long-term goals based on those values. Work with them until they meet most of the ten criteria listed above.

I Value: _____

My Goal: _____

I Value: _____

My Goal: _____

I Value: _____

My Goal: _____

I Value: _____

My Goal: _____

You don't have to be a fantastic hero to do certain things - to compete. You can be just an ordinary chap, sufficiently motivated to reach challenging goals.

- Edmund Hillary

Chapter 30
Mico Staring At The Sea

Motivation

You can't cross the sea merely by standing and staring at the water.

- Rabindranath Tagore

Mico stood there staring at the water. He wanted to cross the sea. He really did. He was tired of his narrow small-town life on this island. He wanted to live on the mainland, to do something different and to learn about new places. Reading about the rest of the world was no longer enough, and though he liked the people he worked with, he didn't want to spend his life working on the docks.

To live on the mainland he would need to find out what kinds of jobs there were, and maybe develop some skills for those. He also would need to save some money. He didn't even know how much it would cost to rent an apartment there, but he had heard it was expensive. This was just one of the many things he needed to investigate and prepare for.

Somehow, though, he just never got started. It wasn't

that he was lazy. He worked hard at his job on the docks, and he was always energetic. But living at the family home was easy, and whenever he thought about what needed to be done to pursue his dream, it seemed like it was beyond him.

He wondered what would happen if he couldn't find a job over there. He imagined the people of the island seeing him return as a failure. He wasn't sure if he could save enough money. He didn't even know where to start. So Mico stared at the sea, and wondered if he would ever cross it.

Motivation Techniques

The best motivation always comes from within.

- Michael Johnson

Do you find that you have a lack of motivation at times? You can learn a hundred ways to improve your life, but then you hesitate to act. Something less important catches your attention, or you just don't feel like doing what you need to do. Even if you are normally a motivated person, there may be times when you have difficulty getting started on an important task, like putting these luck lessons into practice.

There is a solution. Actually, there are many solutions. Here are a few of the best. These are self-motivation techniques that have worked for myself and others. Try them, and if you find even one or two here that work for you, you'll be on your way.

1. **Stop listening to your fears.**

In the story above Mico was afraid, which is normal. But he didn't need to imagine failing, and he didn't have to listen to the fearful voices in his head. He could have doubted his own fearful thoughts, rather than doubting his goal.

Doubt you own thoughts? In the chapter on courage (Dave The Lucky Jerk), we got into how we mistake our fearful thoughts for our own true voice. You don't consider every random thought to be "you," so why not see the worrisome ideas in your mind as just a mechanical process of thinking - one that gives bad advice. Stop identifying with those thoughts.

Call it your "fearful mind" if that helps. Be aware that though it is often talking, you don't have to listen to it. See how the picture it paints is almost always worse than what really happens. Watch how it works to defeat you - not protect you - then you can more easily doubt this part of your mind, so it will lose its power to stop you.

2. **Have a true interest in what you are doing.**

Think for a moment about the most unmotivated person you know. Now consider that he or she gets out of bed and does something - probably every day. Maybe she plays video games all day, or he reads books for hours on end. The point is that we are all motivated, just not always in the direction we would like.

If you have a true interest in your goals, it is easier to do what it takes to achieve them. If your interest is only partial, you can at least concentrate on those parts that are most interesting to you. If you really have no interest at all, it might mean you need to do something else.

~ Secrets of Lucky People ~

On the other hand, if it's just a particular task you dislike, relate it clearly in your mind to the greater goal. I don't particularly like to get up early, but I don't have a motivation problem when I am getting up at four in the morning to go climbing the mountains near here. There are always unpleasant tasks which are necessary when pursuing our passions. As you do them, keep in mind that they are what get you where you want to be.

3. Talk your way into a motivated state.

Tell someone about whatever you are working on that excites you. With a good listener, you will find yourself feeling more energized. This is one of my favorite ways to create energy and motivation. By the time I tell my wife about the book I'm going to write, I'm out of my slump and back at the keyboard.

What if the task itself is less inspiring? In that case, there are two things you can do. You can talk about the larger goals it will help you achieve. This is a way to mentally link the less thrilling task at hand with the excitement of the real goal.

There is also an "energy transfer" technique that works for some people. You can try it when the work in front of you just isn't exciting in any way. You talk about anything else that you are passionate about, and once that gets your energy level up, you get back to the task at hand. You effectively "transfer" that energy and motivation you created.

4. Stimulate your desire.

Imagining a potential future motivates many to sign up for get-rich-quick plans. Good salesmen can put you in your imagined dream home in minutes, and you'll feel motivated to do anything to make it real. Why not learn to be your own salesman?

Visualize the rewards of what you are working on. In the case of these lessons, you might see yourself in the future, being talked about as a lucky person. Find the imagery that gets you excited and make you want to get to work.

5. Stimulate your pain.

An effective *Neuro-Linguistic Programming* technique is to link pain with not acting. This naturally happens when you finally stop hitting that snooze button on the alarm because you think you might lose your job if you wait any longer to get out of bed. The idea here is to use this process consciously.

Imagine any bad consequences that may occur if you don't do what you need to do. Imagine someone who has a really difficult time in life and tell yourself, "that could be me if I don't get to work." Visualize the bad consequences of your failure to act. Essentially you try to make it more painful to do nothing than to start doing what needs to be done.

I have mixed feelings about this one. It certainly seems that positive reinforcement should be healthier for us. On the other hand, we are all different. If a bit of pain gets you going, maybe you should use it.

6. Take any small step in the right direction.

Train yourself to regularly take any small step you can think of that brings you towards your goals. It is a great self motivation technique. There is a momentum created from movement towards a goal. If I commit to raking up one bag of leaves, and start on that, I soon want to finish the yard

~ Secrets of Lucky People ~

work. Of course, sometimes even that small step is hard to take if a goal seems overwhelming. In that case, break larger goals down into smaller goals and concentrate on these.

True story: During a climbing trip, Joe Simpson was left for dead in the Andes mountains, with a broken leg and frostbite. He says he was only able to survive and crawl the three days back to base camp by concentrating on making it to the next rock - and then the next, and the next. He set and achieved hundreds of these short-term goals or steps, and as a result survived against all odds.

I recently watched a movie in which a writer was sitting in front of his typewriter, with the words, "The night was..." He tried adding various words, but none seemed right. We learn that he has been staring at those first three words of his novel for months, frustrated and paralyzed. The obvious solution? Put any word there and get on with it! He could always come back and change it later.

The famous quote, attributed to many different people, says it all, "The journey of a thousand miles begins with a single step." Of course, it has to be followed by another step, and another. With that in mind, consider any place you get stuck to be a new beginning of the journey, and find one more step to take.

Energy Boosters

Sometimes a lack of motivation is due to a lack of energy. I've had problems with fatigue and a lack of energy all my life. It would be wonderful to know why. I've asked doctors, read books, and I have decided that some questions just won't be answered in my lifetime.

Fortunately, I've also learned that even without discovering the root causes of my tiredness, there are always things I can do to alleviate it. The following are some of energy boosters that have worked for me and others. It may help to use several at once.

1. Breath Deeply

Most of us are "shallow breathers." We take in small breaths without using our diaphragm, and a possible result is an oxygen deficiency. Three slow deep breaths through the nose help oxygenate the blood supply better, and especially seems to wake up the brain.

2. Move Around

Often getting up and washing the dishes, walking around the house, or any minor physical activity helps boost energy levels. Just standing up from the computer and stretching for a minute or two can improve how I feel. Tai chi exercises are good for this as well.

3. Listen To Energetic Music

Different types of music have different effects on us, but you can do this one by trial and error. Once you find the ones that work for you, keep them ready. Just recently I finally bought an MP3 player, and I find that having good music that I can carry with me can be very motivating.

4. Try Energy Drinks

The verdict isn't in on most of them, but it's a cheap option to try. I seem to get something from the ones with Ginkgo Biloba. If the drink has caffeine in it, you may want to save yourself the extra expense and skip to number five.

5. Drink Coffee Or Tea

Coffee is the original "energy drink." It makes some of us more tired when it's abused, but short-term, it can work wonders. If you need your caffeine spread throughout the day to sustain your energy, try tea, as it won't give you so much caffeine at once.

6. Get Better Sleep

Our individual needs for sleep may vary from five to ten hours per night. However, beyond a personal minimum, the quality seems to be more important than the quantity. Catnaps work well for some people too, although if they go beyond twenty-five minutes or so, they can make you feel more tired rather than energized.

7. Talk About Something Interesting

This is discussed more fully above. You can even test this technique on an unsuspecting friend. Just get him to talk about something he's passionate about, and watch his energy level rise.

8. Exercise

This is a longer-term solution, but many people notice an increase in their energy level when they get regular aerobic exercise. Personally, I prefer walking, and I find that it also stimulates my thinking. Twenty minutes of aerobic exercise three times weekly seems to be the minimum necessary for a noticeable change in energy levels and health.

9. Take A Hot/Cold Shower

Try a shower with one minute of hot water, then one minute of cold water, alternating for six minutes. This isn't for those with weak hearts, but it will wake you up. Incidentally, research shows that this also revs up the immune system.

10. Get Outside

Sometimes a little sunshine and fresh air can be very energizing. Take your work outside, if you can. Opening a window on a breezy day can help as well.

Of course it makes sense to try to find the reasons for your tiredness or fatigue. However, in the meantime, why not try some of the energy boosters here? None of these are expensive, and you just might have more energy, and motivation, starting today.

Sustaining Motivation

People often say that motivation doesn't last. Well, neither does bathing. That's why we recommend it daily.

- Zig Ziglar

A friend of mine had joined an MLM (Multi-Level Marketing) company years ago, and was very excited. One day he told me about a conference where his "leaders" got all of the distributors yelling and cheering and standing on their chairs. Now, that's a little strange to me (more like a religion than a business) but he was more motivated than I had ever seen him. It lasted a week. He quit the company a couple months later.

~ Secrets of Lucky People ~

Now, I suspect that part of the reason he lost his motivation was because this business didn't really fit his values. It is tough to stay motivated about anything that doesn't really interest you, and isn't very important to you. But the other reason he lost his excitement may have been just what is suggested in the quote above: He didn't work on it regularly.

Bathing doesn't last. What a great analogy. Neither does eating or breathing. There are some things that need continual repetition. Perhaps motivating ourselves is one of those things. So when you learn what works for you, do it again the next day - and the next.

One more quote comes to mind: "Motivation is what gets you started. Habit is what keeps you going." Jim Rohn said that, and it points out the real sustaining power that gets you to your goals. I'll have more to say about habits in another chapter.

Intelligence And Motivation

Some of the most intelligent people lack motivation. This can make their intelligence almost worthless. In fact, because of their powerful intellects, these people have the ability to find the best and most logical excuses for not doing what they need to do to improve their lives.

It is a terrible ability to have.

Of course, we all have this ability to an extent. You can sometimes look at things and see very clearly what all the problems are, right? Exercise this "skill" a bit and soon most goals you might have seem overwhelming. When this happens, why not try looking at things in a different way?

It's easy just to look, right? Without any commitment initially, start looking for specific ways to make your life better, or to work towards some goal. Replace any thoughts about why something might not work with seeing how it could work. Even if you don't accomplish anything immediately, you are preparing yourself. Thinking about change sets your unconscious mind in motion.

Then, when you start to feel the slightest bit of motivation, do something. Take any small step towards your goal. Any action starts the process, and is better than nothing. There is a kind of momentum created by your thinking, and it is maintained by your actions.

Luck Exercise

Try several of the motivation techniques and energy boosters listed above. List three or four that work well for you. You may want to put them on a card in your pocket, or find some other way to remind yourself to use them.

Motivation Techniques That Work For Me

_____

_____

_____

_____

_____

_____

~ Secrets of Lucky People ~

Be miserable. Or motivate yourself. Whatever has to be done, it's always your choice.

- Wayne Dyer

Chapter 31
George's Best Excuses

Taking Responsibility

Blame is a lazy man's wages.

- Danish Proverb

True story: George (not his real name) really knew how to play guitar. There were three others in his band, and they were occasionally paid to perform at the bars in the area. The name of the band was "Blamesong," (not really). They had fun, but unfortunately didn't make too much money, nor did they seem to be getting more popular.

"It's these greedy bars around here," George explained. "They just don't want to pay enough." I mentioned a couple that paid more than the others, and he answered, "Yeah, but they won't hire us." I asked why not, and he explained that the bars didn't think their band was good enough. He blamed the other members for not practicing more.

I asked why they don't have a CD of their own to sell at the bars, like many bands do. It would mean extra income. "We don't have the seven hundred dollars to get a CD made," he explained. I pointed out that they get paid $300 to $400 a night when they play, so they could just set aside two night's earnings to have the CD made.

"I could never talk the guys into that," George protested. He went on to complain about the broken amplifier that caused them to cancel a job (nobody had the money to fix it), and about a bar owner who had cheated them on their share of door receipts for the third time. He had many people to blame for their problems, and he resented any suggestions I had which might take away his excuses.

As you can imagine, the band never did become big and famous. To my knowledge, they're not even playing together any longer. George, by the way, used to comment frequently on his bad luck.

Cognitive Dissonance

Blaming and making excuses are ways to avoid taking responsibility for one's own life. It is a common trait among unlucky people. If you really want to be lucky, you have to overcome these habits. That's what this lesson is about.

When we betray our values, or what we think we should be, we experience what psychologists call "cognitive dissonance." It is the stress that results from holding two contradictory cognitions at the same time. A "cognition," in this context, can be a thought, attitude, emotion, belief or behavior.

For example, if you feel that you're a nice person (or believe that you should be), but you do something cruel anyhow, you experience cognitive dissonance. This uncomfortable feeling must be resolved. Of course, you could admit your wrongdoing and commit to being nicer next time, but usually it is easier to blame the person you are cruel to, and to say "He deserved it." This new belief resolves the contradiction.

The tension is temporarily relieved, but consider what happens when we use blame and excuses to feel better. The new beliefs adopted are based on resolving an uncomfortable feeling, not on seeing the truth. So more often than not, it will be a false belief, because getting at the truth simply isn't the primary objective. As a result, the more we do this, the less we can objectively see reality. We begin to see the world through our own self-deceiving ideas.

Consider George in the true story above. He believed they were a good band, and should make more money. Their lack of success challenged his ideas, creating cognitive dissonance. The resolution? Blame the greedy bar owners who didn't pay enough, or blame the other band members.

The problem with this approach is obvious, isn't it? If there is someone or some circumstance to blame for every failure, and that is all George sees, then in his mind there is nothing to do to make things better. His beliefs have blinded him to any creative opportunities.

By the way, this is true even if most of his excuses cite real facts. The point of resolving one's cognitive dissonance with blame and excuse-making is to get temporary relief from bad feelings. It never is about bettering one's situation. Excuses just don't do that.

Many unlucky people can point out every person and circumstance that is to blame for their bad luck, but they cannot see what their own contribution to their situation is - or could be. Blaming and excuse making is a terrible approach to life. It eventually makes looking for causes outside of oneself automatic. It is difficult for such a person to ever recognize the personal changes needed.

The research on cognitive dissonance is fascinating. For

our purposes, though, you just need to be aware of the process. Try to notice the uneasy feeling that comes when a result you get in life challenges your beliefs or how you think about yourself. When you start to look for an excuse or somebody to blame to resolve that feeling, mentally take a step back instead.

Then look for the truth, and for what *you* can change to make things better. And by the way, it is usually something about ourselves that is most in need of change.

A Closer Look At The Blame Game

Even when based on true facts, does blaming or making excuses for a bad situation motivate us to improve? Not likely. And what do you win when you play the blame game? Not much.

If you could convince others that your parents are to blame for the way you are, what good things would happen? If your business failure could be blamed on something that really wasn't your fault, would that help in some way? Can blaming our personal problems on outside factors ever be helpful?

There is some evidence that assigning failure to things outside our control may be useful for maintaining self esteem and motivation. A good example might be when someone says "Oh, the rain ruined the event," then adds, "I'll have to plan for that next time."

However, many blame the rain without adding the second thought. Of course, the rain does affect events. But the problem with focusing solely on the outside factors that contribute to our problems, is that it's de-motivating, and it doesn't help us learn better strategies for living. What can we learn to do differently when we "prove" to ourselves that a failure was inevitable and outside our control?

~ Steve Gillman ~

Suppose a friend promised to pick you up and give you a ride to a job interview. It is a great job that you really want. He is late, and as a result you never get the job. It is his fault, right? Perhaps, but it actually does no good to dwell on that fact. When you focus on blaming someone else, you diminish your ability to change things.

Here is a better way, a two-step formula:

1. *Learn Your Lessons*
2. *Take Responsibility*

If your friend had an accident, just let it go. It was a one-time unpredictable event, and there usually isn't much to be learned from these. On the other hand, if your friend is always late, you have to learn that lesson, and change your approach. Tell yourself, "I'll get a ride with someone else next time," or "I'll plan to be there thirty minutes early and I'll have a back-up plan." You take responsibility.

Suppose someone stole all your money. They really did something wrong. But why persist in dwelling on what they did? Ask yourself what you can do to make more money, and to keep it from being stolen again. Always focus on what *you* can do, not on what others have done.

It's one thing to recognize when others do something wrong, or storms rain on your parade. It's good to see all the contributing causes. But it's another thing - a useless thing - to persist in blaming outside factors for where you are in life.

Subtle Blame

Never complain and never explain.

- Benjamin Disraeli

~ Secrets of Lucky People ~

Ah, but the blame game can be a subtle one. There is a fine line between the necessary recognizing of "problem factors" and giving control to them. If a person gains weight easily, they have to recognize that fact. Repeating that fact to oneself or others, however, is usually a subtle way of saying, "My body type is to blame, so there's nothing I can do."

To overcome this tendency, include what *your* decisions are when talking about outside factors. Follow, "John just depresses me," with "but I choose to spend time with him, and I can change that." If you catch yourself saying "My parents screwed me up," add "that's why I'm working to change my beliefs."

Have you ever known someone that subtly blames the world for his problems, but never seems to recognize his or her own contribution to them? How happy and successful is he or she? Look closely at the results of blame and excuses, and you'll want to try a different approach.

Everyone of us can think of dozens of people and circumstances that have caused pain or problems in our lives. Who and what are they? Who cares?! What are we going to do about it? That's the important question. Have you ever seen someone blame their way to success? Take responsibility.

Luck Exercise

List a few examples of when you have blamed others or circumstances for your problems or made excuses for your situation or behavior. Then list something better you could have said or done in each case; some way you could have taken more responsibility.

~ Steve Gillman ~

My Excuse: _____

My Better Response: _____

My Excuse: _____

My Better Response: _____

My Excuse: _____

My Better Response: _____

My Excuse: _____

My Better Response: _____

If you have time to whine and complain about something then you have the time to do something about it.

- Anthony J. D'Angelo

Chapter 32
Bad Luck Bart Blames The World

What Unlucky People Do

Some people are so fond of bad luck they run halfway to meet it.

- Douglas William Jerrold

There are two essential ways to improve the good-luck/bad-luck ratio in your life. One is to do those things which lead to more good luck. The other is to stop doing the things which cause bad luck. This lesson is about the latter. It is an examination of the actions, habits and thinking of unlucky people, so that you can learn what to avoid.

Bad Luck Bart

Habit is either the best of servants or the worst of masters.

- Nathaniel Emmons

~ Steve Gillman ~

Bart was waiting for his ship to come in. He dreamt that someday a great opportunity would arrive, and was hoping he would get rich and famous when it happened. It had been a long wait up until this point. Maybe it would happen in time for his retirement years.

While waiting for his lucky day, Bart tried to enjoy life. Unfortunately the things he did seemed to make life less enjoyable, not more. For example, he was deep in debt because of all the things he thought would make life better for him. He was also overweight from enjoying too much food.

He had thought many times about changing his ways. Friends suggested that he start investing for the future, for example, and he liked the idea, but he could only focus on the fact that investments are not entirely predictable. The stock market is up one year and down another. He thought about starting a business, but smarter men than him had seen their businesses fail. "Life is unpredictable," was one of his favorite things to say.

He had hoped that by now he would have met the love of his life. The problem was, as he saw it, that the women he got involved with were unforgiving. He inevitably was unfaithful in each relationship, but he felt that instead of leaving him, the right woman would help him with his problem.

Bart often thought about making money as a disc jockey working at area bars, and his friends agreed that he could do it. He knew about all types of music and had a good voice. The problem was that every time he was close to having some money put together to buy the necessary equipment, he spent it on something that seemed more important at the moment, like a new car or jet-ski. His planning didn't seem to ever extend beyond next week.

Friends were always helping him out. They drove him

to work after his car was repossessed. They loaned him money to make the rent. But their help had limits, and it seemed to Bart that in the end they always let him down.

Some friends did try to offer useful advice. They told him about better jobs, pointed out how he could save money, how he could make his skills into a business, and even what he needed to do differently to have a good relationship with a woman. But Bart was a master at finding the flaws in every suggestion. He was so intelligent he could easily prove that nothing would work.

He was just unlucky, he told his friends. And he could see many of the reasons. They included people who were unfair, and circumstances that had nothing to do with his choices. By fifty years old, he was broke, in debt, living in a small apartment alone, with no real plans or prospects for a better life - but at least he knew it wasn't his fault.

Avoid These Things...

The last chapter covered a couple of the worst bad habits that unlucky people have. Those are blaming and making excuses. Bart certainly was a master at these. Here are some more habits to watch out for.

Unlucky People Wait For Good Luck

Those who are unlucky like Bart commonly say things like, "I'm waiting for my ship to come in." They're very passive in their approach to life. Meanwhile, while they wait, others are out there building ships. Work invites opportunities - waiting doesn't.

To break this habit search out or create your lucky breaks in life. Training yourself to see them can be as simple as looking every day. To train yourself to take advantage of them, always take some small step the moment you recognize an opportunity.

Unlucky People Act On Destructive Impulses

The other day, a man mentioned to me that he had bought a $200 hat. A moment later he said he was hoping they would approve his welfare application. Is this a problem with impulse control, or what? Is it perhaps possible that his bad habits lead to a place on the welfare rolls? In the case of Bart, his impulsive "enjoyment" of life left him deep in debt and perpetually stressed out.

Wait a day before taking any action that commits time, energy or money towards something which isn't a major goal in your life. Do this until it becomes a habit. Probably you'll change your mind by the next day. On the other hand, if you have the impulse to eat something healthy, get some exercise, or pursue an opportunity to better your life - those are the impulses to act on.

Unlucky People Concentrate On Unpredictability

Random events happen, and life is unpredictable, but unlucky people place too much importance on this, using it as an excuse for both inaction and inappropriate action. They see random misfortunes befall themselves and others, and take that to mean that outside factors are to blame for their situation, and there is nothing to do about it. Or they see lottery winners and take that to mean they should buy a ticket, sit back and wait for their "lucky break" to come.

What they don't see clearly, is the predictability within the chaos, and their own role in creating good and bad luck. Think of a casino. Inside, people are randomly winning and losing money. You can't say who will win or lose on a given day. That is unpredictability.

On the other hand, the casino will almost always be a winner, because the rules put the odds in their favor. They can have their ups and downs, but at the end of the year they will have taken in more than they paid out. That's predictability.

Bart is correct when he sees that the stock market might go higher or lower, and that businesses fail. Life *is* unpredictable in many ways. On the other hand, it is easy to predict what will happen to him financially if he does nothing, right? His focus isn't useful at all - it simply excuses inaction and destroys any motivation he might have had to change things for the better.

There is always some way to improve the odds, some way to introduce more predictability into a situation. Lucky people are putting the odds in their favor. That's what this book is about.

Unlucky People Don't Learn From Mistakes

I have a friend who had $30,000 of credit card debt. The payments on this debt alone amounted to almost $1,000 per month. Then there were his other debts, for cars, snowmobiles, and other toys. He only avoided bankruptcy by getting the credit card companies to accept as little as 50% of the balances as payment in full, which he paid by re-mortgaging his home.

What did he do then? Well, with the pressure off, he soon felt comfortable getting a new credit card, and buying a new car. Within a year or two he had more cards. Soon he was deep in debt all over again. Some people just don't learn from their mistakes. They are typically described by themselves and others as unlucky.

There are always "reasons" why doing the same things

didn't work the second or third time around. But the bottom line is that if you do the same things over and over, you will likely get the same results. "Reasons" at this point are excuses, and you can make excuses or you can make your own luck, but you can't do both.

Learn from your mistakes. In fact, always assume that you have some role in the disasters or irritations that befall you, and look for what it is. Identify what you are doing that either causes your bad situations or makes them worse. Then change your approach accordingly.

Even better, learn from other's mistakes and you can avoid making too many of your own. See how others get into trouble and don't do those things.

Unlucky People Think Short-Term

A young man I know paid $750 per month for an apartment when a nicer one was available for $600. Why would he do that? Because he only had $750, and the cheaper place required a $400 deposit. This meant that with the first months rent and deposit, he would have needed $1,000 total to move in - $250 more than he had. Now he pays $1,800 more for rent annually ($150 extra each month) - and probably complains about his bad luck and shortage of cash.

By the way, some might protest, "But if the guy didn't have the money for the deposit, he had to rent the other apartment!" Think! Get creative and think of the larger picture instead of making excuses. If he had to borrow the extra $250 from a loan shark and pay back $500 two months later he would still be much further ahead.

Plan a little further into the future than the two weeks that is on Bart's horizon. Consider for a moment how things would be now if you had done the right things starting years ago? Well, if you do them now, the future can be that bright. Think of the long-term consequences of your actions.

Unlucky People Expect Too Much From Others

Bart seems to think people owe him a living and unlimited help as he repeats his mistakes over and over. Guess what? Except for what you have been promised, nobody really owes you anything. The world is full of generous people, but it is certainly not their duty to help you. Be grateful for the assistance you get, but never be resentful for what you don't receive. It's a self-destructive waste of energy.

If you find yourself feeling like people should help you, stop that thought! Replace it with some thinking on how you can help others, how you can make yourself useful to those you want something from. Giving is the biggest "secret" of receiving.

Unlucky People Are Too Critical

You probably know a person who is an expert in why things won't work. These people can point out the flaws in every plan. They are mostly right too, which makes them all the more dangerous to themselves and others. Their "insight" is a poison that kills dreams.

Lucky Person: "If we do this right, there is a 99% chance of success."

Bad Luck Bart: "So you're saying we could fail?"

It is good to think critically, to see the truth, and so reduce risk. The problem comes when a person sees only the risk and the flaws. For example, this kind of thinking only sees that 70% of restaurants fail, but ignores the other 30%.

If you want to move forward, see the weaknesses in your plan, but to each one add, "And this is what I can do about it..."

Not Everyone Can Be Lucky?

The above is just a sampling of the worst things that unlucky people commonly do. Most of us have a little bit of some of these traits and habits. Fortunately they can all be changed in time, but only if we are willing to do the work necessary. If not, we fall into one of the two categories of people that researcher Richard Wiseman found could not improve their luck:

1. Those not willing to make the effort to change.
2. Those for whom bad luck is an important part of their identity.

What more can I say about the first, except that perhaps the willingness will only come with enough pain to show the need for change. Not much in this book can help improve your luck if you don't apply it.

As for the second group, it may seem hard to believe, but some people get a perverse pleasure out of their bad luck. They say things like, "If it wasn't for bad luck, I wouldn't have any luck at all." They go out of their way to demonstrate how unlucky they are. They're actually proud of it.

Unless they radically change their view of themselves, these individuals cannot become lucky, according to Wiseman. If you identify at all with bad luck, and feel a bit like, "If I didn't have bad luck, I don't quite know who I would be," you need to do some serious work in this area. Believe me, you'll like being lucky even more.

~ Secrets of Lucky People ~

I don't entirely agree with Wiseman's observation, however. Experience tells me that even a person who is proud of his or her bad luck can change it - at least a little bit. This is because some of the techniques in this book work even if you just play around with them. Not all of them are about self-awareness. Some are more mechanical in nature, meaning if you do them, certain results will likely follow, almost automatically.

If you simply spend more time with people, for example, you have a better chance of learning something useful. If you start working in an area that interests you, you are more likely to succeed. Then, when enough good things happen, you can't help but notice it and that will weaken your identification with bad luck.

Luck Exercise

List a few unlucky traits, habits, or attitudes you have at times. Then, after each one, write what you are going to do about it.

Bad Luck Habit: _____

What I Am Doing About It: _____

Bad Luck Habit: _____

What I Am Doing About It: _____

Bad Luck Habit: _____

~ Steve Gillman ~

What I Am Doing About It: _____

Bad Luck Habit: _____

What I Am Doing About It: _____

We rarely acknowledge the role we play in our own bad luck, yet it is self-honesty that brings it to an end.

- Steven Scott

Chapter 33
The Great Ice Cream Opportunity

Luck With Money And Business

A wise man should have money in his head, but not in his heart.

- Jonathan Swift

Perhaps the most common thing people are thinking of when they say they want to be luckier is money. For that reason, I decided to include this chapter. It is strictly about money and business, and how to have more luck with both.

Business Luck

Here's a true story that illustrates several important principles: T. Gary Rogers had just seen his company fail, and though he had virtually no income, he wanted to get back into business rather than look for a job. He liked the idea of an ice cream franchise, so one day he walked into the office of Dreyer's Grand Ice Cream in Oakland, California. He was asking the owner about buying a franchise when a call came in.

The owner soon hung up, almost in tears. The bank had turned him down for the loan he needed to expand the business. Impulsively, Rogers asked him if he had ever considered selling the business. "Not until just now," the owner said. Three days later Rogers had an option to buy the business for one million dollars.

He soon got a group of investors together, took out a loan, and bought the business. It was a big success. (Dreyer's was taken over by Nestlé in 2006.)

Here are some of the things that made this lucky break possible:

- He had courage. After failing at a business and with no income, Rogers still walked into that company office to buy a franchise. Then he had the guts to buy the company.
- He was in the right place. In this case this meant being in the office of the owner, rather than just day dreaming at home.
- He was prepared. He had business experience.
- He paid attention. When he heard the owners phone call with the bank, he saw the possible opportunity and acted.
- He knew the right people. The investors were crucial to this working. He obviously couldn't have done it alone.
- He took a calculated risk. Getting an option to buy the business was a low risk way to buy time to find investors.

There are probably some more "luck lessons" we could glean from this story. For example, the quality of the ice cream sold was undoubtedly part of why Dreyer's did so well. In any case, the bottom line is that Rogers was doing what successful people do.

Change Your Money Beliefs

The better you serve the needs of others, the more money you can make.

- *Steven Scott*

People sometimes have a problem making more money because they have a problem with their beliefs about money. They think that money is "dirty" or "immoral." If you suspect your unconscious feelings and beliefs about money may be holding you back, you may need to change your mind. Let's start with the following explanation.

Many people misunderstand where money and other good things come from. There is the idea that wealth is limited, which is expressed in the saying "a piece of the pie." Wealth is nothing like a pie to be divided up, and it is very important to understand this.

If the wealth of the world was like a pie, if it was a set amount, then of course everything you gained would be at the expense of others. It certainly wouldn't be a very nice feeling to get financially lucky if it meant that an equal share of suffering fell onto others. In fact, the guilt that this idea actually causes may get in the way of many people's success.

Fortunately, this idea is 99% false (almost no idea can be expressed in a way that is 100% true or false). Wealth is not a static quantity of goods or money. It is something forever created and recreated by the mind of man.

The average "poor" person in America today, for example, has cable television and hot water in the shower -

things which were unknown to the wealthiest individuals of centuries past. In fact, there is no unresolvable problem that prevents the whole planet from someday being wealthy. In fact, poverty rates have already been declining for a while now, and it is entirely possible that someday poverty will not exist.

Suppose a potato farmer learns how to produce twice as many potatoes using the same amount of time and land. Suddenly there is more wealth in the world - and it wasn't at anyone's expense. If another person creates art, the potato farmer now has more potatoes to trade for it - or to sell to make money to buy that art. Both men are now richer.

Wealth is created. Understand the value that *you* help create, and you will feel better about it, and the result will be a change in thinking that changes your luck. Even in areas that seem to be zero-sum games, like buying and selling a house for a profit, you are creating value: You are helping a seller and a buyer get what they want.

As long as you do not use force or fraud to get what you want in life, you have to create value to become wealthy. If there is no value created, no person has a reason (nor an obligation) to give you money or other good things in exchange. By definition then, if you conduct yourself honestly, and you get rich, you have created great value in the world. Remember that.

More Money Beliefs To Change

Money was never a big motivation for me, except as a way to keep score. The real excitement is playing the game.

- Donald Trump

~ Secrets of Lucky People ~

There are many good and many bad beliefs out there about money. Some of the bad ones may be holding you back, but you can change them. A few more of these beliefs are listed here, along with better ones which can take their place.

Money Is Bad - or - Money Is A Powerful Tool

You can see how it can be used for bad purposes, but if you look, you'll also see how it is used for good. Concentrate on those examples. Do this enough, and it will start to change your mind about money.

Oh, and by the way, the Bible never says that "Money is the root of all evil." It says that "The love of money is the root of all evil." That's from Timothy 6:10, and it goes on to say that putting money ahead of ones spiritual salvation is the problem. Regardless of faith, you can see that there are things more important than money. That's a good reason to make some - to help us with our higher values.

Money Is Scarce - or - Money Is Abundant

One of the most pervasive and useless ideas about money is that there is a limited amount. This false belief is discussed above, but needs to be reiterated. Wealth is created, and as more real things are created, more money is printed to represent these things.

This is an important point, not just from an economic view, but because people sometimes feel that every dollar they make is making someone else poorer. Unless you make money in unethical ways, the opposite is true. Every dollar you make is making someone richer, because they got something from you that they valued more than that dollar.

~ Steve Gillman ~

Money is more abundant now than ever before, because there are more ideas than ever, which has lead to an abundance of creation of all sorts. Look around and you will see that there is no scarcity of money.

Money Is A Problem - or - Money Is A Solution

Money is only a problem if you make it one. You can choose to use it in ways that cause more trouble, or you can choose to use it in ways that contribute to your most important values. Is money a problem for a child who needs an operation to survive, or is it a solution? Is it a problem for a town which wants a new library, school, or hospital, or is it a solution?

If you feel that money creates problems, look at better examples like the ones above, but also at your own ways of using it. It does tend to amplify the results of habits, both good and bad. If you have trouble dealing with people or with drugs, getting rich can make matters worse. But the problem is personal, not caused by wealth. In fact, money can be part of the solution, even if only by way of a $20 book that helps you see what you are doing wrong.

Money Is A Paycheck - or - Money Is From Many Sources

Many people can't get beyond thinking of money in terms of a paycheck. There is nothing wrong with a job that pays you weekly or monthly, especially if it pays well. But it is very limiting to think only of jobs when one thinks of money.

Money can come from business, of course, but many times people are too limited in their thinking about businesses too. They see only huge investments of time and capital, and so are discouraged from thinking about it further. But a business can be many things, starting even with a few hours invested into free online blog which makes a profit as people click on ads or buy affiliate products.

Investing is another area where people limit their thinking. A bank account can be an investment. A better bank account can be a better one, without much work. Even real estate and stocks can be invested in for as little as $500 with a bit of research.

Think multiple streams of income. The categories "business" and "investment" are each full of thousands of opportunities you may have never considered. Take a look.

Money Talk Is Taboo - or - Money Should Be Talked About

Successful people talk about investing, business, and personal finance. There are always more strategies to be learned, more opportunities to hear about, more knowledge to share and exchange with others. It isn't about obsessing on money, but about recognizing what an important part of our lives it is. We talk about health issues because they impact our lives so profoundly, so why wouldn't we talk about money as well?

Not talking often leads to relationship problems, especially when a couple has different ideas about how to make and spend money. A lack of communication about these issues can lead to all sorts of financial troubles. If you believe or feel money is a taboo subject, find people who have healthy conversations about it. Listen, and ask questions.

~ Steve Gillman ~

Money Is Only For Others - or - Money Is For Me

Sometimes people feel that money is just something they aren't meant to have. If you have this belief, look at people who have come from similar circumstances as yourself and still learned how to make and manage money. See how they did it. See how you might do it. Start the process of learning what you need to learn, and note any minor successes you have. This will provide the evidence necessary to convince your unconscious mind that money is for you.

Business Is Dirty - or - Business Is Noble

Some see business as taking advantage of people. Individuals in business do treat customers unfairly at times, but that is a recipe for failure, not success. Consider the salesman who is "so good he could sell ice in the arctic." No matter how persuasive he is, he will probably sell that ice just once. Soon after he will suffer the consequences of not properly serving others.

Business serves people, and profit is the reward for doing it well. It's about giving all of us what we need and want. When a company doesn't properly serve consumers, it fails (unless governments exclude competition). In other words, they try to serve the people's best interest as defined by the dollars those customers spend. Some may do this only to make a profit - but a free market still forces them to think of how to best serve others.

Business is about honesty. Not all players are honest, but we often learn about the dishonest ones when their companies dramatically fail. Honesty is very good for bringing customers back. In other words, it pays, as good business people know. A truly free market encourages that.

All the products and services we value, from medicine

~ Secrets of Lucky People ~

to wonderful music to paper and food - it all comes by way of business. Someone had to use their mind, money and resources to figure a way to provide everything we need, and all that is asked for this service is a price we are willing to pay (if not, we wouldn't pay it, right?). So when you think of business, try to see it as the noble pursuit it is and can be.

Luck Exercise

Identify and write down several money ideas or feelings that may be holding you back. Then write down a better belief. Finally, look for and note any evidence for your new beliefs.

Questionable Money Belief: _____

A More Useful Belief: _____

Evidence: _____

_____

Questionable Money Belief: _____

A More Useful Belief: _____

Evidence: _____

_____

Questionable Money Belief: _____

~ Steve Gillman ~

A More Useful Belief: _____

Evidence: _____

_____

Money is only a tool. It will take you wherever you wish but it will not replace you as the driver.

- Ayn Rand

Chapter 34
The Unlucky Expert On Luck

Develop Lucky Habits

The day you decide to do it is your lucky day.

- Japanese Proverb

Angie read every self help book out there. She could quote a hundred authors and explain everything from "manifesting" to secret motivation techniques to six ways to cure a bad habit and six hundred ways to improve oneself. She even read a book on how to get lucky.

Unfortunately, she was still working at the same job she hated, five years after starting there. She was still getting involved with men who didn't treat her well, and still renting a small apartment and driving a car that was in need of repairs which she couldn't afford. Anxiety filled her days and nothing seemed to go her way.

Angie knew why, of course. In fact, not only could she give all the reasons for the way her life was going, but she also knew all the things that could be done to make it better. She was an "expert" in self improvement and success - at least in her own mind. After all, she had read more books on these things than anyone she knew.

One day Angie told her friend Andrew about the book on how to get lucky. There are dozens of ways to bring more opportunity into one's life, she explained. He asked for examples, and listened carefully as she gave him three. Then he asked her if it worked. She quickly said that the book was "fascinating" but that she hadn't had time to try out the techniques in it yet.

Andrew thought about the simple ideas she had explained from the book. He decided to put them to the test. He was working too hard at his job delivering furniture, and his wife was making barely over minimum wage as a cashier. He was ready for a change.

First, he remembered what Angie had said about being in the right place for luck. Both he and his wife had always wanted to buy a house, and maybe even get into real estate investing. He made a list of what were most likely the "right places" to help with these goals, and soon went to the first one on the list, a local real estate office. He returned many times, to ask about new listings and get advice.

He started to habitually pay attention to conversations around him, and to look for opportunities in what he heard. This was another technique that Angie had told him about. He took notes too. One day, while he was at the real estate office, he overheard some agents talking about "staging" a house.

"What is staging," he asked. The woman explained that people put furniture and decorations in empty homes to help them improve the look and feel, so they sell more easily. That gave Andrew an idea.

He knew how to get cheap high-quality furniture, because the store where he worked always sold returned pieces for half or less of their original price. Other stores did the same. Of course, he knew how to move the furniture - that was his job. His wife had an excellent eye for decorating. Perhaps "staging" houses could be a good business for them.

The third lesson had to do with how to overcome fear. Andrew had been practicing the techniques Angie had explained, and so he found it possible to finally start taking the steps necessary to start a business. He asked his boss to cut his schedule to four days per week while keeping his pay the same, instead of giving him the raise he was supposed to get. The time that was freed up went into starting the business.

His wife loved the idea. They did their research, and soon had business cards printed up. They ran through all their credit cards buying furniture and decorations, which they stored in his brother's garage. When Andrew overheard a friend say he was selling his empty rental house, so he offered to "stage" the home for free for the first couple weeks, in order to take photos for their portfolio.

With this first job under their belt, Andrew distributed their business cards to all the real estate agents he had met, some of whom recommended his service to home sellers.

By the following year his wife was able to quit her job to work full time on the business. Andrew worked at his job for a few months more. By the third year they were making more money than ever. They had bought a new home as well, and were saving money to invest in real estate.

Meanwhile, Angie was still working at the same job, even though she hadn't received a raise in pay for more than a year. She bailed her latest boyfriend out of jail one day, and the car broke down as they tried to get home to the same crowded apartment she had been in for years. It seemed that her bad luck would never change.

She wondered about the success that Andrew was having. It didn't seem fair. Angie missed the obvious truth: she may have known all the secrets, but his habit of using just three of them was more powerful than any amount of mere knowledge.

Habitual Luck

Motivation is what gets you started. Habit is what keeps you going.

- Jim Ryun

To put it all together and get lucky on a regular basis, you have to take the lessons here and make them into habits. As with most techniques and ideas like these, if they're not habitually used, they're not very useful. Consider how forgotten and worthless is some of the knowledge from your childhood school lessons, because it was never used. On the other hand, you still can read, write and do math because you have used these skills repeatedly.

So what should you do for better luck?

Do The Exercises To Create Lucky Habits!

Start with the "Luck Exercises" at the end of each chapter. There is a lot to do there, and some of the exercises will take weeks to complete. But you don't have to do them all at once. Pick out the ones that you think will help you the most, and start with those.

Refer back to these lessons if you are not sure you understand what an exercise is for. You may want to read it several times in any case. Repetition helps memory. Also, if you read it again a month or a year from now, you'll have had experiences that make you say, "That makes more sense now!"

~ Secrets of Lucky People ~

Self improvement "experts" will tell you that it takes about three weeks to develop a new habit. Maybe so, but we are all unique in some ways, so take as much time as necessary. Although most of the specific techniques here can change things for the better if you simply use them today, making them into habits is well worth it. Once you put in the work, habits make life easy, and in this case, full of good luck.

We first make our habits, and then our habits make us.

- John Dryden

Chapter 35
A Collection Of Luck-Boosting Ideas

Life is "trying things to see if they work."

- Ray Bradbury

Here are some quick suggestions on how to be luckier. They're those techniques and thoughts that don't require a long enough explanation for a chapter of their own. You may want to read through the following ideas more than once, and put them to use one at a time.

Curiosity

Lucky people are probably more curious. There isn't much research on this, but it makes intuitive sense. The more you explore the world around you, the more likely you are to make a fortunate discovery or two.

My wife Ana and I love to drive down the dirt roads here in Colorado. Some of them are certainly rougher than our car should be exposed to, but that's just the part of the price of curiosity. The reward is the occasional beautiful waterfall, pond, or interesting cave that we find. Our friends sometimes comment about how many interesting hidden places we know, but they would know just as many if they were as curious as we are.

The next time you see a friend or acquaintance who is excited about something, ask about it. It might be something you could be excited about too. If you see a new and interesting business in town, stop to check it out. There might be an opportunity there, either to buy something that can enrich your life, or to get a new idea for your own business.

Have you ever seen something going on in a park or the parking lot of a mall and wondered what the event was about? Why not stop and see next time? We did once and found a radio station giving away submarine sandwiches and coffee mugs. Good timing since we were looking for something to eat. Make time in your schedule for satisfying your curiosity.

Play To Your Strengths

Many years ago, when I worked at a casino, the floor employees (dealers) had a fifteen minute break every hour. This provided enough time during a shift to gamble in the break room. I was lucky, according to some there, because I always won more money than I lost. But why?

It was simple. The employees there gambled on everything from backgammon to checkers to card games. I just played chess, and occasionally poker - if it was the type I was proficient at. I bet on both. Knowing what I was good at, I avoided the other games. I never liked gambling, as most of them did. I just liked winning money.

You'll have more luck in life if you play to your strengths. For example, if you were opening a new restaurant with a partner, you should ask yourself if you're a better entrepreneur or manager. Split up your duties accordingly. Want a good deal on your next house? Who is the better negotiator, you or your wife?

Let her handle the offer if that is where her strength is. But if you understand finance better, then get involved in choosing the mortgage loan. Learn where your strengths and weaknesses are, and use that knowledge to your advantage.

Teach Good Luck Techniques

Want to really "set" these lessons in your mind? Teach them to a friend or family member. There is nothing better for learning something effectively than teaching it to someone else.

In the process of putting thoughts into words to teach another, you are telling yourself the logic behind what you think, feel, or partly understand. Often, explaining a thought *is* the process of understanding. In addition, any repetition or explaining of material helps you remember it better.

No student available? You can always study as a teacher. This can totally change your perspective and make your learning more efficient. Simply keep the idea in mind that you'll be teaching what you're learning. Imagine how you'll teach it, even hearing the words you'll use.

Be Decisive

People hesitate to act until their dreams die in old age - and then they wonder at their bad luck. Learn to be decisive if you want to be luckier.

What happens when you can't make up your mind? You feel stressed out, perhaps even miserable if the decision is an important one. But that is just the short-term ef-

~ Secrets of Lucky People ~

fect. The worst part is that every time you refuse to make a decision, you strengthen this stress-causing habit. You are training yourself to do less and have more anxiety.

For this reason alone a bad decision is often better than doing nothing. You can often immediately resolve the stress when you finally decide to sell your car, buy that exercise machine, or write that letter. Nothing can crowd and cloud your mind with worry quite so much as decisions waiting to be made.

Go ahead and make that decision, and if it proves to be a bad one, make a new one. Did you know that many missiles are fired with barely any aiming? They simply adjust course as they go, and they still hit the target. "Ready, fire, aim" is the process, and it works in our personal lives too.

Of course there are times when it is too soon to make a choice about something. In those cases you can still make minor decisions, like setting a deadline for the major one, or deciding what to do about smaller parts of the problem, or choosing to set aside the problem until a future date. The point is to consciously address the issue, rather than letting fear or a habit of procrastination keep you from doing anything.

Worried you'll make bad decisions? Well, you will. That's the price of success. Entrepreneurs fail an average of three times before succeeding. And what about non-entrepreneurs? They don't fail at business - but only because they never decide to have one.

Study Luck

Ever find yourself saying, "That sure was lucky?" Ask why. In fact whenever you see something lucky happen in someone else's life, see if you can identify any factors that contributed to their "luck" (or success, if you prefer). Then imagine how you can apply what you learn. Then apply it.

Planned Spontaneity

The idea that you can plan spontaneity seems contradictory to most people. It isn't really.

For example, years ago a friend called me up to see if I wanted to go to North Carolina the next day. He was going to visit a girlfriend, but we could explore some caves on the way, and I could go backpacking for a few days in the Smoky Mountains. The whole trip would be about two weeks.

I agreed right away, and had a great time. I was able to test out the lightweight backpacking gear I had recently bought, and test some outdoor survival ideas I was curious about. This, in turn, eventually helped with the construction of my backpacking web site - my third best revenue generator among our sites.

What made this spontaneous decision possible? Several things that I very consciously planned. Money in the bank, for starters. Secondly, I had the idea in my mind that I wanted to take a trip, and so I had a packing list ready. At the time, I also had a job which I could easily take time off from. In other words, I was prepared to be spontaneous.

You might not have the same situation as I had, but you can plan in little ways to be spontaneous. And the benefits are more than just fun. Consider the success of my backpacking web site. Spontaneity leads to opportunities.

Suppose you are going out to eat, for example. You think you will be out for two hours. Why not set aside five hours just in case something interesting comes up? Also be sure to have some extra cash on you. If no interesting opportunities present themselves, nothing is lost. You had a nice dinner and got home early.

~ Secrets of Lucky People ~

On the other hand, what if you met a friend who was on his way to a seminar on how to trade stocks for a living. If you didn't have the time or money, you could do nothing more than wish him well. However, if you planned for the unexpected, you are able to make a spontaneous decision to join him. You may learn something useful, or get to know someone who will help you in the future.

What are the easiest ways to allow for more spontaneity in your life? Try these:

1. Put a lot of "free time" into your schedule.
2. Have some extra money available at all times.
3. Watch for opportunities to do something spontaneous that you might enjoy and benefit from.

Learn The Skills To Maintain Luck

It is sometimes amazing to people from other cultures how many wealthy people in America have been both poor and rich several times in life. The financial culture of the United States is very dynamic. You can make money more easily than in many countries, but you can lose it easily as well.

If you want to continue to be lucky in life, you need to learn the necessary skills to manage the luck you have. It is wonderful to get lucky in business or investing, but not so fun to lose it all and have to start over again. You need to learn money management skills to keep what you make, and to make it grow into more.

You also have to learn time management skills. As more good things start happening in your life, it will be more difficult to make time for everything. Prioritizing helps, but you also have to learn to use your time most effectively on the things that are your priorities.

Start studying! Read a couple good books on these subjects now, and you'll thank yourself later. What if you don't?

A True Story

There once was a woman who won a million dollars in the Michigan Lottery. It was being paid out to her over twenty years, which meant that she received $50,000 per year, or a little over $3,000 per month after taxes. This was a lot of money in the 1980's, and she was generous in sharing it with her friends. How lucky she was, they thought.

She started having regular parties for friends every month when the check arrived. She also got new furniture from the rent-to-own place. She bought a new Cadillac. But soon she was in trouble. Between the parties and the payments on things, the money seemed to be gone almost as fast as it came in. It wasn't long before she was starting to lose the things she had bought.

How do I know this story? Because at the time I was a "repo man." I repossessed people's cars in the middle of the night when they didn't make their payments. In fact, I took her Cadillac. All of her money was spent soon after the check came in each month, and then when the payment was due on the car, she couldn't make it.

Yes, I repossessed a car from a million-dollar lottery winner. I guess it wasn't her lucky day. It isn't enough to have some good fortune - you have to learn how to manage it too.

Nice People Get Lucky

It might be no surprise to discover that nice people are luckier. Luck, after all, often comes by way of others, and is more likely if those others like us. But luck isn't just in what happens, but in what doesn't happen.

For example, if you're a doctor, you might consider it unlucky to get sued, and very fortunate if this never happens. So what's the best way to avoid lawsuits? Being nice.

In one study, doctors were tested to determine which are more likely to be sued (important research for malpractice insurers). Not making as many mistakes in treating patients helps reduce the risk of a lawsuit, but guess what? Being nice helps a lot more. The study showed that friendly doctors who spent more time talking to their patients were far less likely to be sued, even if they made more mistakes than others.

People rated as "nice" are 50% less likely to divorce, according to a study at the University of Toronto. A study at Rutgers University shows that they make more money for the companies they work for. Researchers at the University of Michigan found that those who volunteer time for various causes live longer than those who don't. Bottom line? Being nice has it's advantages.

Identify Essentials

Learn to identify the most essential elements of a situation or opportunity and you'll have more good luck. Let's look at my own experience with our internet business as an example.

Early on, my wife and I knew nothing about the internet. We understood that you could put up a web site and sell something or get paid for "clicks" on advertising links. We got a basic page builder that wasn't even sold any longer, but it was enough to start making our little web sites. They were less than perfect, to be generous.

Other sites had nice images and flashy designs. Ours

were plain by comparison. It is embarrassing to admit, but we didn't realize for over a year that we could center the pages instead of having them stuck off to the left.

However, our plain pages started to make money, even as we watched flashy web sites fail. Why? We concentrated on the essentials. In this case, that meant getting traffic to the sites, having good information that made the visitors want to stay, and having some way to make money from the visitors.

I understand the value of having a more "professional" look. Our own web sites improved in appearance as we learned more. But the bottom line in our business is: Traffic plus good content plus good products and marketing equals profit. Putting these things ahead of learning PHP (still don't know it), or how to have a clock on the page, or any other "extras" like that, is what helped us succeed.

When you look at a situation where there might be some opportunity for you, ask "What is essential here?" Ever watch a single young man plan and think about how he is going to approach some woman? Typically, he'll think of all sorts of non-essentials. Meanwhile, another man walks up to the woman and does the essential thing: he says hello.

Delay Gratification

There have been several studies done on delayed gratification and its relationship to success. One of the first was at Stanford University, where they put kids in a room with a piece of candy in front of them. The children were told that they could eat it now or wait fifteen to twenty minutes and get two pieces to eat. Only one third of them waited and received the two pieces of candy.

14 years later the researchers followed up. Those chil-

~ Secrets of Lucky People ~

dren who had been able to delay gratification were found to be more emotionally stable. They also scored higher on their SAT tests. Essentially, they were better prepared for life.

You'll notice a common trait among unlucky people. They don't wait for things. They have to have everything now, which - among other negative effects - means credit card debt and the stress that follows.

Being able to delay gratification means you get more in life. For example, when paying cash you don't pay interest, and you often get better deals. This means you have money left over to buy other things. Another example: If instead of buying things now and working long hours to pay for them, you wait, work less, and use the time to develop skills and knowledge, you'll soon be able to produce more income - and have more things.

Of course self discipline doesn't sound like much fun to many people. It doesn't have to exclude having a good time, though, and it certainly doesn't mean you have to plan every step of your life. For more about that, see the section on "Planned Spontaneity" above.

Dealing With Negative People

Keep away from people who try to belittle your ambitions. Small people always do that, but the really great make you feel that you, too, can become great.

- Mark Twain

Maybe you have a friend who continually hints that you can't succeed at this or that. Or one who has to point out the negative aspects of every proposal. Then there are those people who are just plain bitter and seem to want the world to join them in their misery.

What can you do about the negative energy emanating from these people? First of all, recognize that it isn't always just that person. Often it is the way you interact with them. A critical person might even be useful to have around if intelligent analysis is what you need at that moment. On the other hand, such a person may drain your energy if you waste your time defending yourself from their petty and unnecessary comments. Ignore them or ask them to stop!

Fortunately, there are other ways to change the negative energy between you and another. One way is to talk about something positive that the two of you have a common interest in. This often dissolves the negativity.

Another simple technique is to ask the person for some good news. Push the person to tell you about anything that is going well in his or her life. It is hard to maintain a negative feeling when talking about something good. Try this one; it really does work most of the time.

If the above techniques don't work, or if the person is just always depressing to be around, the solution is simple; spend less time with that person. Of course you have to spend some time with unpleasant people. They may even be those you love. You have no obligation to take part in their negative thinking, though, and you can reduce your exposure.

Do Luck Lessons and Exercises Work?

You may have noticed in the book that I mention the research of scientist Richard Wiseman several times. In the course of his studies he ran a "luck school" which taught students how to be lucky. How well did the students do?

Almost every participant in Wiseman's "school" reported significant life changes. These changes included:

~ Secrets of Lucky People ~

- More good luck
- More self esteem
- More confidence
- More success

In other words, if you put these principles to work, they really do increase your luck. Maybe this is a good time to do those exercises again?

Life Is Less Expensive For Lucky People

Lucky people are opportunistic and open minded. This result is that they get to pay less to have the same things as other people. How does this work? Let's look at an example.

Suppose a man wants a new boat, and he has his mind set on getting a particular model. He is annoyed when the salesman tries to tell him about another boat. He buys the boat he wants for $13,000.

Now you come in looking for the same model. The salesman also mentions the other boat. You listen, and learn that the other is very similar, but it was a repossession. The previous owner had used it perhaps twice before being unable to make the payments. In other words, it is almost new.

It becomes obvious that the salesman really wants to sell it. You look around and realize that this boat dealership doesn't carry any other used or repossessed boats. You ask and find out that this employee sold the boat originally, and is feeling some pressure to get it off the lot. After a little negotiation, you get the boat for $8,000, with the original two year warrantee in place.

You get essentially the same thing for $5,000 less. Why? Because you were open minded and looking for opportunity. If you had insisted on getting exactly the boat you thought you wanted, you would have paid more, like the other customer did. Now you have $5,000 left over to spend on something else, or to invest in your future.

This is just one example of how the traits of lucky people help them spend less and get more. With a little imagination you can see how any one of the principles in these lessons could lead to lower-cost opportunities.

Slow Down

One day I noticed that when I am obviously in a hurry, and moving fast, the person at the checkout counter of the store rushes to ring up my order. I suppose you could see this as a subliminal technique to use when you want to speed someone up. But I don't want to cause more stress for others, and I miss a lot when I'm rushing. I miss the opportunity to talk to people, and to notice things around me that may be worth noticing.

When I purposefully slow myself down, I learn useful things. For example, I felt like rushing through our closing on the house when we moved to Colorado, but I made myself slow down and talk to the others present. In the course of the conversation, one of the real estate agents mentioned a secret swimming hole, out of town and a mile down a small trail, where we could jump from the cliffs into the water. We found it a week later and it was one of the more beautiful spots we have been to.

Try slowing down and talking to others, or just looking around. You might just get lucky.

Look For Advantages And Take Them

This is such a simple idea, yet most people just don't

~ Secrets of Lucky People ~

make it a habit to think, "where is there an advantage here?" I used to occasionally bet on chess games, but I made it a point to play against players who were not as good as me. Seems like an obvious idea, but what about all the players who were sitting across from me losing game after game? Apparently it didn't occur to them.

At a casino which had poker tournaments, players were allowed to choose the table they sat at, and there were generally six per table. After a round, the two top winners from each table went on to the next round. The rest were out of the tournament at that point.

Many nights the tournament wasn't full, so there were two or three tables with only five players. Two players would still be going on to the next round, so what should you do if you were just arriving and choosing where to sit? Well, two-out-of-five is certainly a better probability than two-out-of-six. It seemed that almost none of them recognized this simple advantage.

Always look for an advantage you can take. If you are making an offer on a house at the same time as another buyer, what can you do to get yours accepted? Maybe you can close sooner, if that is important to the seller. Maybe you can offer a little more, or offer better terms if the seller is financing the sale.

This is about turning problems into opportunities as well. What advantage is there in having a job that requires an hour commute each way? How about the opportunity to listen to 400 hours of audio books annually. That might teach you something useful.

This also means looking for the easier way to do things. Buy clothes which don't need dry cleaning and you save yourself from a regular errand. Shop during off-hours and you avoid the crowds. There is almost always a better, easier way to do something, or some advantages to be had.

Start looking for them.

More Inspiration

Here are some of great quotes on many topics that relate in some way to "luck" or whatever we call the good results we get in life. Each suggests something which, if we think about it, will teach us a "life lesson."

Life shrinks or expands in proportion to one's courage.

- Anais Nin

Small opportunities are often the beginning of great enterprises.

- Demosthenes

Knowing others is intelligence; knowing yourself is true wisdom. Mastering others is strength; mastering yourself is true power.

- Lao Tzu

We can't solve problems by using the same kind of thinking we used when we created them.

- Albert Einstein

You can have everything in life that you want if you just give enough other people what they want.

- Zig Ziglar

~ Secrets of Lucky People ~

Besides the noble art of getting things done, there is the noble art of leaving things undone. The wisdom of life consists in the elimination of non-essentials.

- Lin Yutang

Better be wise by the misfortunes of others than by your own.

- Aesop

We are all self-made, but we usually only say it about the successful.

- Steven Scott

There is more to life than increasing its speed.

- Mohandas K. Gandhi

Formal education will make you a living; self-education will make you a fortune.

- Jim Rohn

Failure is simply the opportunity to begin again, this time more intelligently.

- Henry Ford

Man cannot discover new oceans unless he has the courage to lose sight of the shore.

- Andre Gide

~ Steve Gillman ~

Imagination is more important than knowledge.

- Albert Einstein

He is able who thinks he is able.

- Buddha

A Final Note

Sometimes things really do just happen, for better or worse. But the next time you find yourself saying "She sure is lucky," or "He gets all the breaks," look a little deeper to find some reasons why, and perhaps a lesson to apply.

Go and wake up your luck.

- Persian Saying

(the end)